# MYSTERIES AND LORE OF WESTERN MARYLAND

# MYSTERIES
## AND LORE OF
## WESTERN MARYLAND

*Snallygasters, Dogmen and Other Mountain Tales*

SUSAN FAIR

THE
History
PRESS

Published by The History Press
Charleston, SC 29403
www.historypress.net

Copyright © 2013 by Susan Fair
All rights reserved

First published 2013

.

ISBN 9781540208408

Library of Congress Cataloging-in-Publication Data

Fair, Susan.
Mysteries and lore of Western Maryland : snallygasters, dogmen, and other
mountain tales / Susan Fair.
pages cm. -- (American legends)
Includes bibliographical references.
ISBN 978-1-62619-024-5 (pbk.)
1. Folklore--Maryland, Western. 2. Folklore--Maryland--Frederick County. 3.
Monsters--Maryland, Western. 4. Monsters--Maryland--Frederick County. 5.
Ghosts--Maryland, Western. 6. Ghosts--Maryland--Frederick County. 7. Haunted
places--Maryland, Western. 8. Haunted places--Maryland--Frederick County. I.
Title.
GR110.M3F35 2013
398.209752'87--dc23
2013025758

*What sort of bedlam am I about to encounter?*
T.C. Harbaugh

# Contents

# CONTENTS

# Acknowledgements

I extend my gratitude to all the folks who helped me in many different ways with this project, including Joy Allison; Doug Bast; Mary Bender; Patrick Boyton; John Bryan; Heidi Campbell-Shoaf; the Carroll County Public Library; Dave Dull and Antietam Cable Television; Lori Eggleston; Rob Fair; Mannie Gentile; John Hoptak; Dwight Hutchinson; Linda Irvin-Craig; Ike Mumma; Tom Riford; Bob Study; Reverend Robin Swope; Dianne Wiebe; Emily White; Jake Yohn; two of my favorite buddies in weirdness, Andrew McCormack and Larry Phelps; and the nice folks from the Maryland Room at C. Burr Artz Public Library.

# Preface

On November 19, 1833, a newspaper in Cumberland, Maryland, told of a strange and terrifying event:

*On the night of Tuesday last, the 12th inst., a most alarming and awful sight was witnessed by many of the citizens of this city and county generally. The whole heavens were illuminated, as far as the eye could penetrate, with what is commonly called "shooting stars." They flew in every direction, like snow in a storm, except from the earth. Some of them appeared as large as a half-bushel, with every variety of size from that down to a spark of fire, with brilliant tails, corresponding in size with the ball they followed. At times they were so thick that the whole atmosphere appeared in flames. Many of them came within a few inches of the earth before they vanished...It commenced about twelve o'clock, and only disappeared by the light of the sun after daybreak.*

We can just imagine the folks in Western Maryland stumbling out of their homes into the cold darkness, gazing with fear and wonder at this night of falling stars, wondering, perhaps, if the end of the world was upon them.

What people in Western Maryland witnessed that night in 1833 was what is now known as the Leonid meteor shower, though in a form rarely seen—one so strong it's usually called a storm rather than a shower. But to those early Marylanders, it was the unknown and nothing short of terrifying.

The Great Leonid Meteor Storm of 1833 is depicted in this engraving by Adolf Vollmy. It is based on an original painting by Karl Joslin. *From Wikimedia Commons.*

And so it goes with many things we doesn't understand. Sometimes, we invent stories to explain these things, and sometimes, these stories are both wonderful and bizarre. Western Maryland—the counties of Frederick, Washington, Allegany and Garrett—were born of a very stouthearted and imaginative people who were faced with some unique hardships. Perhaps that is why, today, Western Maryland has some of the most unusual and fantastic folklore of any region in the United States. And some of these wonderful tales continue to unfold.

In keeping with the spirit of the wonderful Western Marylanders, the tone of this book is often light. The book is far from comprehensive; each county has enough stories to fill volumes and volumes of its own. In *Mysteries and Lore of Western Maryland*, I have tried to take a new look at some old stories and to bring to light other tales in danger of being overlooked or forgotten. The book also celebrates some unique Western Maryland locations and characters.

Each of these stories is part of a bigger story. They're reflections of Western Maryland's singular interactions with war, prohibition, racial issues, disease and death, as well as love, family and home. They're explanations, they're hopes and they're morality tales.

To deal with the adversity, challenges and changes they all too frequently encountered, Western Marylanders developed their own recipe of fortitude, creativity, an appreciation of nature and a sense of humor. These qualities helped shape Western Maryland into what it is today: a culturally diverse area with amazing natural resources, captivating history and awesome people. I still experience a thrill each time I return home to see the familiar and evocative mountains loom into view.

So come travel with me for a very different look at Western Maryland. The tour starts here.

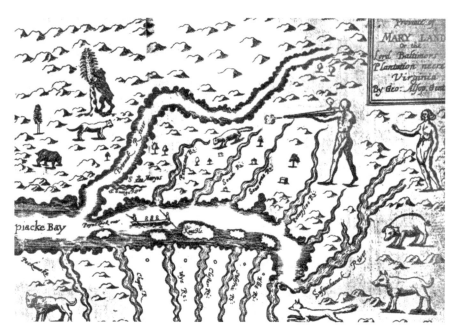

George Alsop came to Maryland as an indentured servant in 1658. In his 1666 book, *A Character of the Provence of Maryland*, he provided this peculiar hand-drawn map showing some of the animals found in the state. Monster enthusiasts have sometimes speculated about the creatures he depicts in Western Maryland. *From* A Character of the Provence of Maryland.

# Part 1

# Western Maryland Monsters

*My, I'm dry! I haven't had a good drink since I was killed in the*
*Battle of Chickamauga!*
*—the monster known as the Snallygaster, quoted in the*
Middletown Valley Register

The monsters of Western Maryland are a hideous reflection of just what it takes to tame a new frontier and live through uncertain times. Some of these creatures are furry, fanged and fearsome. Some are fire-breathing fiends that fly. Some almost defy description, and some are all too real. So pack a lunch, fire up your cellphone camera and follow me through time as we pay a visit to Western Maryland's twisted menagerie. Take a deep breath: things are about to get beastly.

# The Snallygaster

## *The Monstrous Misadventures of a Mountain Menace*

Imagine waking up to the news that a giant winged creature had swooped down and seized a man walking along a road before carrying him off, sucking out all his blood and tossing him aside like yesterday's chicken bones.

That's just what happened to folks who opened the *Middletown Valley Register* on February 12, 1909. The article was accompanied by a letter from a man in Casstown, Ohio, who claimed to have spotted a "gigantic monster" called a Snallygaster a few days earlier and warned that it appeared to be heading toward Maryland. And either the folks in Western Maryland were unusually impressionable or there really was something terrible on the loose, because within hours of its first appearance in the *Register*, people in Frederick and Washington Counties and even in nearby Shepherdstown, West Virginia, began reporting encounters with the flying monster.

And what a monster it was: the dragonlike fiend was said to have huge wings, a long pointed tail, occasionally a horn, one eye in the middle of its forehead and, strangest of all, octopuslike tentacles that trailed behind it like streamers and retracted like a cat's claws. Many reported the creature as sporting razorlike talons, although one woman said she saw hoofs. While descriptions of the creature varied fabulously, two things remained consistent: it flew, and most alarmingly, it seemed to be in search of its next victim.

One of the most unnerving Snallygaster encounters was reported by a fellow named George Jacobs, who claimed he not only saw the creature while he was out hunting but also took a shot at it. It was at that point that poor George discovered two very unpleasant things. First, the bullet merely ricocheted off the creature, and second, the monster apparently didn't care for being shot at. As a matter of fact, it was so annoyed that it pursued Jacobs across a field, all the while lunging angrily—or perhaps hungrily—at the terrified man's neck. The community shuddered.

The *Hagerstown Mail* chimed in and reported that the Smithsonian was interested in studying the Snallygaster. But according to the *Middletown Valley Register*, it was probably going to have to settle for a dead specimen: that newspaper announced that the military was sending in troops armed with a Gatling gun. And furthermore, the paper added, big-game enthusiast President Teddy Roosevelt was planning to get involved; after all, who wouldn't want a Snallygaster head mounted over his mantle?

In a scene reminiscent of *Jaws*, trigger-happy locals went monster hunting. At least one large owl was a casualty of the Snallygaster frenzy. The wounded owl was imprisoned in a Myersville basement while gawkers, intrigued by headlines like "Snallygaster Captured," dropped by to take a gander. That, they decided was no monster, and sure enough, the captive owl was vindicated when Snallygaster sightings resumed. When last heard of, the unfortunate owl was slated to be mounted as a trophy.

The Snallygaster was undeterred by these threats of violence (or, more likely, it simply wasn't a reader of the local newspapers), and it proceeded to do one of the most curious things ever attributed to a one-eyed, flying reptilian monster. After some hijinks near Cumberland that involved terrorizing a man working at a brick kiln and sucking down the entire contents of a large tub of water intended for a boiler, the Snallygaster announced to the astounded worker, "My, I'm dry! I haven't had a good drink since I was killed in the Battle of Chickamauga!" This bizarre disclosure implied that the Snallygaster was somehow the reincarnation of a soldier killed during the Civil War, a circumstance that just might be without precedent in all of monsterdom.

Before long, the papers reported another alarming development: the Snallygaster had laid eggs. Some industrious Sharpsburg men said that they had acquired an egg that the creature had carelessly deposited in a barn and were keeping it in an incubator. What their plans were once the egg hatched was anyone's guess.

Meanwhile, the Snallygaster's reign of terror was about to come to a screeching halt. The capricious monster had decided to pay a visit to a train station in Emmitsburg. There, it spied a railway worker named Ed Brown, swooped down and snagged him by the suspenders. Another local man bravely tried to save Brown by grabbing hold of the victim's foot as the Snally attempted a frantic takeoff. Fortunately for Mr. Brown, his suspender was no match for all this, and it broke. He fell to the ground but not to safety—Snally wasn't giving up that easily. Soon, another man joined in the fray, and in a flurry of flying fists and flapping wings, the men proceeded to battle the Snallygaster for over an hour. Several other locals, one of them armed with a gun, also joined in the fight, and it was at this point that the Snally exhibited one of its more fantastic skills: shooting fire through its nostrils. According to the paper, Norman Hoke, an Emmitsburg deputy game warden (there really was a Norman Hoke living in the area during this time) pulled out his badge and, Barney Fife like, ordered the monster from the county. At last, Snally had had enough. The winged menace turned pointed tail and took off for some nearby woods. Actually, it must have been really tired of all the fuss the citizens of Western Maryland were making because the great and fearsome Snallygaster would not be seen again for another twenty-three years.

During the more than two decades that the Snallygaster slumbered (or, perhaps, vacationed in a more hospitable clime, possibly one where the people didn't make such a big deal about a little bloodsucking and fire-breathing), the monster was relegated to local-legend and good-way-to-scare-the-kids status. Mom-friendly threats like, "Oh, Billy and Betty, get in here for supper before the Snallygaster gets you!" were said to be employed with great frequency. But the Snallygaster, it seemed, wasn't finished with Western Maryland.

In early November 1932, new reports of Snallygaster sightings began coming in, and this time, they spread far and wide—even national newsman Lowell Thomas did a piece on his radio show in December.

Seen gliding about in the skies of the South Mountain area, this Snally, it was speculated, was likely the offspring of the creature that had terrorized the valley in 1909. Obviously, it was surmised, a Snallygaster egg takes about twenty-three years to hatch, and now the time had come. A young, energetic Snallygaster was on the scene of its parent's old haunts. This new generation beast was equipped with sensational color-changing properties, according to witnesses, and seemed to be biding its time. It had to be up to something. Sure enough, a few weeks later, this celebrity Snallygaster embarked on the adventure that resulted in its demise. And true to its over-the-top persona, it went out with a bang—or rather, a splash.

On December 21, Hagerstown's *Morning Herald* featured the eye-catching headline "Death of Snallygaster Is Reported: Accounts Differ." The article referenced the *Middletown Valley Register*, which told the fantastic story of Snally's last adventure. As you will recall, Snallygasters tend to be a thirsty breed, and apparently, this particular Snallygaster was not a fan of Prohibition. It paid a visit to notorious moonshine hotspot Frog Hollow in Washington County, presumably in search of a bit of liquid refreshment. According to the *Register*, the Snallygaster was lured by "fumes arising from a 2,500 gallon moonshine liquor vat." That was a lot of hooch—so much, as a matter of fact, that the monster was "overcome and fell directly into the mash." The still's five attendants were said to have vamoosed, leaving the still and the Snallygaster in the hands of a Prohibition agent and a sheriff's deputy who had happened by, seeking not monsters but moonshiners. These officers, George T. Danforth and Charles E. Cushwa, were not only named in the *Register* as being on the scene, but Danforth was also quoted as saying, "Imagine our feeling when our eyes feasted on the monster submerged in the liquor vat."

George Danforth was an actual agent in Hagerstown at this time, and Charles Cushwa was a sheriff's deputy. The connection of these two very real gentlemen to this story implies that one of two unlikely things must be true: either there really was a Snallygaster found drowned in a vat of moonshine in

## Scene and Incident of Snallygaster's Reign

—Courtesy Baltimore Post.

### Bovalopus Dies By Same Hand Which Caused Existence

(Continued from Page 1.)
Danforth, in charge of the Hagerstown prohibition office, accompanied by Agent Charles E. Cushwa, who had received information concerning the big moonshine plant, arrived in Frog Hollow Thursday morning, and much to their surprise, they found the plant abandoned. But imagine their feelings when their eyes feasted on the monster submerged in the liquor vat. With a feeling of trepidation the two men cautiously made their way to the vat and were greatly relieved to find the monster cold in death.

A hasty examination by the two agents revealed that the mash had eaten practically all the flesh from the

Edward M. L. Lighter.

Let us whisper it girls, but the man who writes the best love letters doesn't necessarily make the best husband.

**READING NOTICES.**

Charles F. M

northwest of Myersville conveyed unto the said J by deed from Cyrus F. Fl bearing date the 2d day 1909, and recorded in Li 302, Folio 58, one of the of Frederick County, sa

The *Middletown Valley Register* published this eye-catching article documenting the Snallygaster's alleged demise in December 1932. *Maryland Room, C. Burr Artz Public Library.*

Washington County in 1932 or Prohibition agents had a really good sense of humor. I'll leave it up to the reader to determine which is more likely.

In any event, even though nothing remained of the poor Snallygaster except its skeleton (its flesh had been eaten away by the "large amount of lye" in the moonshine), the agents weren't taking any chances. They promptly secured five hundred pounds of dynamite, placed it under the vat and blew the Snallygaster and the moonshine to kingdom come.

The events of 1909 and 1932 obviously beg the questions: where did the story of the Snallygaster originate—and why?

The *Frederick News Post* said that the first written report of the monster appeared in 1902. At that point, it was supposedly called a "crosswise gyascutus." What the *Post* didn't indicate was where this written report appeared because it wasn't in the *Post*. The Snallygaster that took flight from the offices of the *Middletown Valley Register* in 1909 did so at the pens of a reporter named Ralph S. Wolfe and the paper's editor, George C. Rhoderick. It seems, however, the newspapermen didn't dream up the Snally on their own.

It's likely no coincidence that just a few weeks before the Snallygaster appeared in the Middletown Valley, another monster was putting on quite a show just a few states to the north: the Jersey Devil. Like the Snallygaster, the Jersey Devil was a winged pain-in-the-neck that had been putting in appearances in the Garden State since the 1700s. Rhoderick and Wolfe, noting the interest and newspaper sales the Devil drummed up in New Jersey, could very well have decided to scare up a winged creature of their own. Of course, the Snallygaster and the Jersey Devil could also have been one and the same. This particular rash of Jersey Devil sightings ended in mid-January 1909, allowing a pretty reasonable time for a winged creature to make a leisurely trip from Jersey to the mountains of Maryland.

There has also been speculation that there was something a bit more calculated involved in the Snallygaster's emergence. Some think the beast may have been born of local uneasiness with the proximity of the National Road; they say the Snallygaster could have been a scare tactic aimed at hobos and other ne'er-do-wells passing through. Warning them they could become dinner for a ravenous monster might have seemed like a pretty good way to keep undesirables from loitering around town. And later, in 1932, the Snally could have reemerged to worry moonshiners.

The Snallygaster has also been accused of being born of something quite a bit more sinister. It's been said that the dangerous monster was first invented after the Civil War to frighten freed slaves and continued to be used to keep local blacks "in their place" or, at least, keep them from being too comfortable in the Middletown Valley. The first victim of the Snally, who was thrown off the hillside, was a black man named Bill Gifferson, according to the *Register*, and the headline of that first Snallygaster article read, "The Colored People are in Great Danger."

Yikes.

Furthermore, a similarly named monster, the Snoligoster, had already made an appearance in the cypress swamps of Florida. It had supposedly impaled an "outlaw Negro" on a spike on its scaly back. In spite of this murder, the monster was allowed to live unmolested because "the very report of such a creature inhabiting the swamps would deter evil-doers from venturing into these wild places to avoid their pursuers and escape justice."

While we let this distasteful information sink in, let's also consider explanations of a more cryptic nature. Those Snallygaster descriptions (though maybe not the fire-snorting or octopus tentacles) are reminiscent of the long-extinct pterodactyl. Some believe the extinct species could have survived in the dark woods and caves of South Mountain. It's even been reported that the Snallygaster was added to the state's endangered species list in 1982, though the Maryland Department of Natural Resources says there is no record of Snally ever making the list. Of course, that could just mean the DNR knows something we don't—maybe there are so many Snallygasters out there it's not in danger of becoming extinct at all.

A final thing to consider about the origins of the Snallygaster is who informed the paper of the original sighting. The random letter in the *Register* from the man in Casstown, Ohio, who predicted the Snallygaster's venture into Maryland was none other than T.C. Harbaugh.

Thomas Chalmers Harbaugh was born in Middletown in 1849. His family moved away when he was a small child, but Tom visited Middletown often throughout his life—when he wasn't busy writing those 650 "nickel novels" he authored, that is. The fact that Mr. Harbaugh, who published under many pseudonyms, maintained an interest in Middletown and its lore was evidenced by a book his wrote in 1910, *The Middletown Valley in Song and Story*. During those yearly visits he paid to Middletown from his home in Casstown, one would assume he spent time visiting his best friend, George Rhoderick, the editor of the *Middletown Valley Register*. According to Rhoderick, Harbaugh's "facile pen did more to memorialize Middletown and Middletown Valley in both prose and poetry than perhaps any other one agency in all of their history." As a matter of fact, Harbaugh was a regular contributor to the *Register*, and not long before the Snallygaster story broke, an article celebrating Harbaugh's sixtieth birthday was featured on the front page.

# Harbaugh Seen By Sketch Artist, Surrounded By Products Of His Pen

Thomas C. Harbaugh, aged poet and writer of fiction, has returned from Casstown, Ohio, to this county, and is now residing at Montevue Hospital, where he expects to spend the remainder of his life.

Yes, it appears that T.C. Harbaugh could be a missing link in the evolution of the Snallygaster. Who better than a writer of serial novels and a chronicler of local legends to help a buddy out by dreaming up a Maryland mountain monster for his newspaper?

The imaginative Harbaugh, by the way, made a good living from writing all those novels. Sadly, assisted by several friends (one of them being Rhoderick), he returned to Maryland to live in the poorhouse when his health failed him and his fortune dissipated. There, he amused reporters and visitors with wild tales before being shipped back to Ohio, where he died in 1924.

But really, the folks of Western Maryland deserve recognition. All it took was one little story, and local residents—not to mention reporters and editors of competing newspapers—were ready to release their inner monsters, collaborating on a creation that gleefully took on a life of its own. You can hardly blame folks for wanting to be distracted, too, because there was something else scary making its way around Western Maryland in 1909 besides stories of giant, flying monsters. The Maryland State Tuberculosis Sanatorium opened in Frederick County that year. If you had the disease and wanted to be admitted, you only had to be three things: a resident of Maryland, not a "hopeless case" and white.

Whether the Snallygaster was the offspring of a bored newsman and his dime-store novelist friend, the monstrous personification of a changing community's fear or its desire to inspire fear in certain segments of the community is hard to say. It also makes one wonder what it meant that they created this beast only to then kill it off.

Perhaps there is a small chance that residents really did see something monstrous up there in the skies of Western Maryland. In the saga of the Snallygaster, a real monster just might have been the best-case scenario.

## The Snarly Yow Stalks the Mountain

Another monster is known to have stalked Frederick and Washington Counties—this one in the 1800s—and the residents of South Mountain had seen this particular creature so often they assumed it was a real animal.

*Opposite*: T.C. Harbaugh came home to Frederick County, where he was expected to live out his remaining days in the poorhouse. While there, he entertained everyone with his fanciful and presumably rambling stories. In 1923, Frederick's *Daily News* published this sketch showing the author lost forever in a fantasy world of his own creation. *Maryland Room, C. Burr Artz Public Library*.

A real animal, that is, with a mouth full of fangs and a disconcerting ability to assume gigantic proportions. An animal capable of bringing on strange hallucinations in those who encountered it, all while being impervious to blows and bullets. You know, that kind of real animal. Let's go see for ourselves!

When Madeleine Dahlgren was documenting the folklore of South Mountain—that tangle of forests at the crossroads of Washington and Frederick Counties, which somehow manages to be beautiful and foreboding at the same time—in the 1800s, she was struck by the frequency with which the beast she came to call the "Dog-Fiend" appeared in local stories. But she was even more interested in the fact that the locals seemed not to question its existence any more than they did the presence of the mountain's bears, deer and rattlesnakes.

But the Dog-Fiend was no ordinary animal. The fact that this creature, so casually accepted by the locals, was not only called the Snarly Yow or the Black Dog but also sometimes referred to as "the Werewolf" speaks volumes about the fortitude of these folks. In her 1882 book, *South Mountain Magic*, Dahlgren wrote of the local attitude toward the Snarly: "They have therefore supposed it to have been some wild animal whose habitat has never been properly explored." She described a typical encounter with the creature, given to her by a man she called "a credible witness—a good type of a sturdy mountain man." The witness, whom she called "William L——e," was supposedly returning from nearby Boonsboro late one night when the Black Dog loomed in the darkened roadway in front of him. Whether the man really encountered a monster, had a pathologically overactive imagination or simply invented the best excuse ever for staying out late at the tavern, the reader will have to determine, but here is William's story as related by Dahlgren:

> It was clear starlight and the ungainly form of the beast could be distinctly traced. It was black, and bigger than any dog he had ever seen; and, as he came nearer, the object intercepted him, and stood guarding the road in such a way as to forbid his crossing. So, to use his own expression, he "fit him." That is, nothing daunted, he fought at him. But, to his confusion, as the creature was attacked, it "grew longer," and presently seemed to extend across the road, making no noise, but showing a very wide and very ugly-looking red mouth; while, all the time the thick and heavy blows rained down upon it, the sinewy arm of the woodsman met with no resistance, but rather seemed to beat the air.

A farmer's wife who got a good moonlit look at the beast as she rode by in a sleigh reported that it was "much larger than any dog she had ever seen." But even stranger than its size was the weird, somewhat hallucinogenic effect sighting the Snarly seemed to have on viewers. One man claimed to have been "seized with a sort of color blindness" upon seeing the creature and reported that he saw it change from "coal black" to white. And a farmer encountering the Black Dog

# Beware of the "Snarly Yow"
Legend has it that the shadow of a black dog used to prowl the heights of South Mountain. One night, a huntsman, famous as a sure shot, encountered the beast. He aimed and fired his rifle. The shot went right through the animal with no effect. He fired again and again, each shot passing through the shadowy beast. Finally, overcome with dread, the huntsman fled.

"Beware of the 'Snarly Yow'" warns this wayside marker along alternate Route 40 in the South Mountain region. The road was once a favorite path for the menacing dog creature. *Mannie Gentile photo.*

was overcome with the sensation that "the hill was coming down upon him." Assuming the travelers along South Mountain's winding roads weren't stopping to sample some sort of magic roadside mushrooms, this was one freaky monster.

The Snarly Yow seemed to be quite a creature of habit. According to Dahlgren, "In all the narratives concerning this vision that we have heard, substantially the same course is mentioned." This path just happened to cross the National Road, which is why, naturally, there were so many sightings. And this is also why, to this day, travelers can have their very own Snarly Yow sighting if they choose. For the Snarly has a very unusual distinction for a monster: his likeness adorns a historical wayside marker along this very road—today known as Alternate Route 40—just outside Boonsboro and across from Old South Mountain Inn, once the dwelling of Dahlgren herself. "Beware of the 'Snarly Yow,'" the marker warns ominously. Travelers might do well to take heed because even though the wily creature usually has the sense to avoid what is today a very well-traveled road, every once in a while it seems he is overcome by nostalgia for his halcyon days as a public menace. Bewildered motorists on South Mountain will occasionally report striking a very large dog with their vehicle, only to watch the beast mysteriously dissolve into the moonlit night.

# DWAYYOS AND DOGMEN

## *Werewolves of Western Maryland*

*Dogman in the Headlights.* This Scherenschnitte (or cut-paper) image by Maryland artist Robinson Fair depicts an encounter with the creature known as the Dogman. *Courtesy of Robinson Fair.*

It's probably not the kind of e-mail your average man of the cloth receives, but in 2009, when Robin Swope, a minister in Erie, Pennsylvania, received a message from a young woman he called "Aubrey" that related a very strange and horrifying experience she'd recently had in Frederick County, Maryland, the good reverend took her very seriously. The reason he didn't dismiss her weird claims is because Swope, in addition to being reverend at a Church of Christ in Erie, is what he likes to call a "Paranormal Pastor." For Swope, being a paranormal pastor involves "investigating the unexplained with a distinctive Christian perspective," a calling that includes writing books, articles and blogs about paranormal topics; speaking at conferences and on national radio shows, such as *Coast to Coast*; and, occasionally, having people come to you with really chilling stories.

The story Aubrey related to Reverend Swope was no run-of-the-mill ghost encounter or demonic possession. Poor Aubrey, it seems, ran into a real, live monster along a back road in Frederick County. The creature she saw was what is (in some circles) commonly referred to as a "dogman," and this dogman, like oh-so-many dogmen (apparently), was quite an unpleasant character.

Aubrey told Reverend Swope that she had been on a nighttime drive to a friend's house, taking her time navigating the tree-lined, winding country roads outside Gambrill State Park in Frederick County, when she began to feel a strange sense of dread. Aubrey said she inexplicably just didn't feel safe; even so, she slowed her car down to a crawl.

That's when she saw it. At first, it was just a blur, something large and brown flickering in and out of the trees alongside her vehicle. Oddly, even though whatever it was remained just inside the woods, it seemed to be keeping pace with her slowly moving car.

Then, horribly, the thing wasn't in the woods anymore.

All at once, like a figure from a nightmare, it bounded out of the shadows, and there it was: a huge doglike beast, standing on two legs, its mouth a grimace of sharp fangs and hatred. The creature looked right at her with dark eyes, and then, as if on cue, it growled and leapt toward her car.

Aubrey hit the gas, and her last sight of the beast was of its outstretched, grasping claws.

As you can imagine, Aubrey was badly shaken up by the encounter, and as you can also probably imagine, people don't tend to take reports of sightings of werewolf-like beasts very seriously. So it's no wonder she turned to Reverend Swope with her story.

And here's something else to keep in mind: Aubrey's experience wasn't the first time a strange, aggressive, bipedal doglike creature had been sighted in Frederick County. In November and December 1965, the front pages of the county's newspapers were filled with stories about an upright walking monster that became known as the Dwayyo.

It began with the headline "Mysterious 'Dwayyo' on Loose in County" on November 29, 1965. The article related a curious tale: a man named John Becker had contacted the local Frederick paper the *News* to report not only that he had seen an upright-walking, six-foot-tall black dog but also that the creature had attacked him. The *News*, in turn, reported the whole thing to the local police. There were, of course, a few loose ends. The police stated that they couldn't locate John Becker or the road, Fern Rock, where he supposedly lived. And as for the name "Dwayyo," well, it was not readily apparent where that had even come from. But all that was soon beside the point. The story of the Dwayyo had legs—big, furry, muscular ones. A hunter near Middletown soon claimed he had seen a Dwayyo, too, and a little boy reported to the *News* that he saw them "everywhere."

Throughout December 1965, the *News* coyly played both sides of the fence on the dogman tale. First, it published a sketch by a newspaper artist and labeled it "the Dwayyo." The sketch depicted a tall, thin, doglike animal standing upright and sporting an unusually long and bushy tail. It was accompanied by an article containing quotes from Frederick residents saying, well, some kind of smarmy things about their neighbors who had seen the Dwayyo, such as this sarcastic comment: "I think the person who called that story in must have been getting into the holiday 'spirits' a little too soon."

As the month progressed, the story continued to develop. It was discovered that Fern Rock Road did indeed exist; it was said to be a small, off-the-map dirt road just outside Gambrill State Park. And Dwayyo stories continued to emerge. A local woman blamed the Dwayyo for the strange noises she heard outside her mountain home at night. "It cried like a baby," she told the *News*, "then screamed like a woman for months. All our neighbors heard it." And a Jefferson woman saw one chasing a calf. The *News* was soon proclaiming, "The Dwayyo could become this area's most famous monster."

The local police had their hands full with the Dwayyo story. A man phoned the station and announced he was keeping a baby Dwayyo in his basement; upon arriving at the address given by the caller, police were greeted by a very confused man who didn't have a baby Dwayyo in his basement, or anyplace else, but apparently did have some pretty devious friends.

Meanwhile, the mysterious John Becker reemerged, this time via a letter to the newspaper. He admitted to using a pseudonym to protect his privacy but insisted the Dwayyo encounter had been all too real. He gave more details of the incident: "It was as big as a bear, had long black hair and growled like a wolf or dog in anger," he said. "Becker" reiterated that he had fought the monster until it finally took off and disappeared back into the woods surrounding his home near Gambrill State Park. And, he said, he had several other witnesses: his wife and children.

Lair of the dogman. This rural road in Frederick County was the scene of a recent dogman sighting. *Photo by Mannie Gentile.*

Perhaps inevitably, the paper soon announced that a "Dwayyo Hunt" was being planned. The hunt was apparently instigated by students at the local community college and high school, and up to one hundred people were said to have signed up. How this almost comically large posse planned to find the Dwayyo and what they planned to do with it in the unlikely event that they did find it turned out to be moot points because there is no evidence that the great Dwayyo Hunt ever came off.

The Dwayyo articles reached a pinnacle of silliness on December 15, 1965, with the publication of a poem contributed by a local woman that began "Santa's coming in on a Dwayyo." Turned out the dog-monster, according to the poem, would be filling in for a sickly Rudolph, so the author pleaded, "Please don't hurt the Dwayyo."

The Dwayyo outbreak of 1965 eventually fizzled, but Frederick's dogmen continue to emerge from the shadows in the form of strange sightings such as the one "Aubrey" reported, and a similar one, of a bipedal wolflike creature that startled two men in the Catoctin Mountains in the 1970s. And in case you're wondering, Reverend Swope does believe that Aubrey saw something very strange along that Frederick County roadway. He wonders if dogmen sightings could be linked to a tradition sometimes associated with indigenous cultures: shape-shifting. He explains, "Tradition tells us that after a journey to the spirit world where the shaman defeats certain enemies he is given powers to transform into his spirit guide animal, and sometimes more than just one. They can be any animal but the famous ones are the Wolf, Bear, and Crow in North America."

While it's time for us to leave the somewhat disturbing world of the dogman and get to know some other Western Maryland monsters, keep this in mind: if you happen to encounter a strange, upright-walking doglike creature in Frederick County, don't try to pet it, don't try to pick a fight with it and, whatever you do, please don't try to hitch it to a sleigh.

## BEWARE THE JABBERWOCK

### *Frederick's Own Chupacabra*

In the April 30, 1887 edition of Frederick's *Daily News*, sandwiched between a description of the weather in Middletown and a notice for a Feast of St. Joseph church service (for which the decorations, we are advised, "though not elaborate, will be very fine") was this curious piece of information:

> *A correspondent of Wolfsville, this county, relates that a gentleman of that place had an exciting experience with the now famous and fearful "Jabberwock" on Sunday night last, on the road leading from Foxville to Wolfsville, and rumor has it that his gait would have done credit to the flying Dutchman. The young man's descriptions of the noises he heard are truly fearful and it is thought that he will never be caught on that road between two days again.*

"Beware the Jabberwock, my son! The jaws that bite the claws that catch!" So cautioned the poem by Lewis Carroll, and in Frederick in the mid- to late 1800s, these words were taken very literally. When Lewis Carroll included his nonsensical poem "Jabberwocky" in *Through the Looking Glass* in 1871, little did he know that he was spawning a series of monsters across the ocean—or at least providing them with a really cool name.

There are several peculiar things about the Frederick creature known as the Jabberwock (as if something called a Jabberwock could be anything but peculiar). One interesting thing is that there was not just one but at least five separate creatures that went by the name Jabberwock in Frederick history. It seems as though the name was the favored go-to moniker for miscellaneous monsters in the 1800s, and while Jabberwock may not be a genus of monster unto itself, at least one of the variations sounds suspiciously like a certain creature that gets a lot of press today. And here is another very unusual Jabberwock tidbit: one of the incarnations of this particular monster favored the downtown area of Frederick. As you may know, city-dwelling monsters are usually underrepresented in monsterdom, so this fellow is really quite remarkable.

Unlike the Jabberwock that terrorized the hapless traveler on that dark, rural Frederick County road, the Jabberwock that made its home in downtown Frederick seemed to enjoy the city life—or maybe it just enjoyed having a denser population to menace. According to a 1932 reminiscence in the *Frederick Post*, many Frederick residents carried guns, and everyone locked their doors and windows during the downtown Jabberwock's reign of terror in the early 1870s. Said the *Post*, "Tales went about concerning a horrible face that would peer into the countenances of startled and horrified persons residing in the vicinity of McMurray Street and nearby sections." Children, the memoirist noted, screamed on merely hearing the name Jabberwock.

Descriptions of the Jabberwock were a bit sketchy but seemed to focus on the beast's mesmerizing eyes. Folks "claimed they had never beheld such eyes." Others thought the urban beast was "a stalking animal unlike any even zoologists would recognize." The downtown Jabberwock was said to be unusually tall, and it scaled fences like a high jumper, "while persons residing in the houses watched spellbound." Police gave pickpockets and brawlers a little breathing room and instead sought the monster. Several gun-wielding locals fired off shots at the Jabberwock, and finally, one of the bullets found its mark.

According to the paper at least a thousand people viewed the dead Jabberwock in a vacant lot on West All Saints Street. What they saw made them shudder as they jostled for a better peek. It was a "huge, queer looking and unsightly species of dog of such proportions that it may have been a great Dane or mastiff, but peculiarly marked and with a face that in the dark would have terrified the bravest heart!"

The descriptions of the dead downtown Jabberwock hearken to another beast of legendary mystery and homeliness: the chupacabra. Could this Jabberwock have simply been a very large, very mange-ridden dog? The residents of Frederick were sure they had slain a monster, as the *Post* boasted, "All bad little children as well as the good ones could fall asleep peacefully at night, neither fearing for their young lives nor caring anymore more about *jabowaks*."

Yet another Frederick creature dubbed the Jabberwock put in appearances 1890 in the area referred to as "Creagerstown to Graceham to Thurmont." This version of the Jabberwock was unflatteringly described as "lizard-headed, humpbacked, long-tailed, and web-footed." Then, in 1895, something called a

Jabberwock got ink in the July 27 edition of the *Daily News*, in a section quaintly entitled "The Girl About Town: Things Told About in Her Tour of the Metropolis," the "metropolis" being, apparently, Frederick County. In this case, the female reporter, "Mary Jane," was told about a decidedly hideous monster. "Liberty has a sensation," she glibly related, "a Jabberwock has appeared and startled the natives. It is hard to tell what it is, Barnum's what-is-it is nowhere beside it. But it strikes me that it is a creature of unknown origin surveying for the electric railway." Quite a wit, that Mary Jane. Maybe you had to live in a rural area in the 1890s to get that joke.

This brings us to our last and possibly most notable Frederick Jabberwock—notable because this guy was a real animal owned by an enterprising Frederick resident. He dubbed his creature "the Frederick

A vintage postcard depicts a Frederick City street at night; the creature called the Jabberwock was said to roam downtown Frederick in the 1800s. *Author's collection.*

Jabberwock," and it was intriguingly described as a "combined sheep and calf." (In this case, the possibility of a serious birth defect seems the most pleasant explanation for how someone happened to have a half-sheep, half-calf creature.) Yes, this gentleman, known as James Hill, aka "the peanut man" (no explanation given, although we can assume he sold treats to go with his one-monster sideshow), had his very own "Jabberwock," and he was only too happy to show it to you—for a price, of course. An announcement in Frederick's *Daily News* on July 19, 1887, stated, "James Hill and his Jabberwock have returned from a trip through the county and the latter is now on exhibition at the summer-garden, 6ᵗʰ Street and Klinehardt's alley." Sadly, the coup of the alley show notwithstanding, events were about to take a tragic turn; a few days later, the same paper announced the bad news: "James Hill, the peanut man, is in mourning for the loss of the famous Frederick County Jabberwock, which he had hoped to sell to P.T. Barnum. The animal expired Sunday." RIP little Jabberwock, whatever you were.

# Reptilian Troubles

## Hoopsnakes, Rattlers and Other Rascals

The worst thing about the reptilian troublemakers famous for terrorizing the mountains of Western Maryland is that most of them were real.

Western Marylanders of the 1700s and 1800s had to deal with a lot of scary things: bears, wolves, numerous wars taking place on their doorsteps and, of course, that awkward situation with the Indians. But just when they thought it might be safe to take a stroll through the mountains or lay their heads down for a well-earned rest, snakes—and plenty of them—slithered into the picture. As a *Harper's Monthly* correspondent who visited the area in 1879 commented, "The snakes were powerful abundant. South Mountain was full of 'em—black-snakes, copperheads, moccasins, and rattlesnakes." A local historian writing during the 1800s also made note of the almost snake resort–like atmosphere of the area: "The black-snakes, moccasins, and copperheads…sun themselves in the centre of the highway."

And so I have now come to that part of the tour that causes some to squirm: what I like to call the Western Maryland Reptile House. And no, I won't make fun of you if you choose to wait on the bus.

Let's hit a few of the herpetological highlights. Our first exhibit is the black snake. Also called the rat snake, this fellow can grow to over six feet. Usually, the rat snake is the leave-'em-alone-and-they-won't-bother-you kind of reptile. In Western Maryland, however, the black snakes seem to be endowed with powers of super-pestiness. Case in point is a story related by Madeleine Dahlgren in the 1800s:

> A woman told us that, walking up the Mountain canyon one bright moonlight [sic] night, she felt something tugging at her dress. She walked on for some time without giving the matter much thought, until a nearer rustling noise caused her to look around, when she saw two large black snakes clinging to the hem of her dress. She was compelled, as she expressed it, "to give battle," in order to shake them off.

Our next exhibit is the timber rattlesnake. The timber rattler bears the rather appropriate sounding Latin name *Crotalus horridus* (which translates to something like "ghastly earrings"). The good news is they are still around today, though not as plentiful as they apparently once were. Kind of a win-win for snake lovers and ophidiophobiacs.

So just how plentiful were timber rattlers back in the day? Famous Garrett County outdoorsman Meshach Browning, whose hunting heyday was the early 1800s, claimed to have killed thousands of them. Not thousands of snakes—thousands of rattlesnakes, which, in case you did not know, are venomous. And Meshach, rugged as he was, was more than a little creeped out by the plentiful snakes. "I was so much afraid of the serpents that I did not like to be out after night," he admitted. Meshach went to quite a bit of trouble to keep the plentiful serpents off his person:

> *Before leaving home I always took hay, or long grass, and twisted it into a large rope, with which I wrapped my legs up to the knee; and this they never could bite through. When thus provided, I would go where I pleased in daytime; but being afraid they would creep to me in the night, if I was where I thought they were numerous, I would stuff leaves round my legs, inside of my pants, and sleep with my moccasins on; and making my dog lay down, I would lay my head on him; knowing then no snake or animal could take me by surprise.*

As if the poisonous venom and the annoying rattling weren't bad enough, the Western Maryland rattlers were also notorious pigs. Meshach once saw one with a full-grown rabbit bulging in its middle and described another swallowing a groundhog.

Early Western Marylanders were pretty much used to dealing with worst-case scenarios, and snakebites were no exception. This was the procedure for dealing with the inevitable poisonous snakebite, as documented by a historian in 1906:

> *If an unfortunate person was bitten by a rattlesnake or a copper snake the reptile must be killed at all hazards and was cut in sections about two inches long and laid on the wound to draw out the poison. The pieces were then gathered up and burned. Afterwards an application of boiled chestnut leaves was made.*

Meshach Browning had a more enticing remedy. A snakebite victim should be made to drink "from a pint to a quart of whiskey which will not

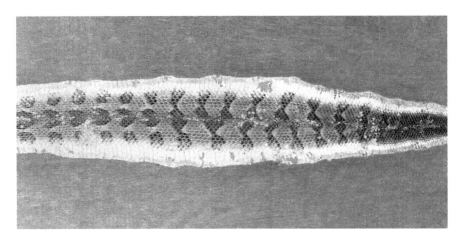

Reptilian folk art. This skin from a South Mountain rattlesnake has been mounted on a board for display. *Courtesy of the Douglas Bast Collection.*

intoxicate the patient, but will neutralize the poison." He didn't mention what his treatment for alcohol poisoning was.

As if it wasn't bad enough that early Marylanders had to deal with a remarkable number of run-of-the-mill poisonous rattlers and copperheads, there were also, if tales are to be believed, other more unexpected and alarming serpents on the prowl. And so I give you the "Western Maryland Strange Serpent" exhibit.

In *South Mountain Magic*, Madeleine Dahlgren related tales the locals told her of a species of "hooded viper" that could cause death by blowing on its victim with poisonous breath. "A man killed one on the cliff back of South Mountain House," she wrote. She also documented local tales of the dreaded hoop snake. If you don't know what a hoop snake is, this description from one of Dahlgren's sources, an "old mountain woman," pretty much sums it up:

> *The hoop snake puts its tail in its mouth, when in pursuit of its victim, and rolls on with an incredible rapidity. The reptile wears a horn on its head, and kills whatever it touches!*

Dahlgren related the old woman's personal experience with the horrible hoop snake. While walking on South Mountain, she and some friends saw something green stretched out in the grass. They stopped to examine the object when suddenly "it put its tail in its mouth, raised its horn, and began to roll." The group managed to jump up onto a fence out of its way but watched it rolling downhill, leaving a slimy trail in its wake. They swore that a tree that the hoop snake had touched on its way down the mountain withered and died.

The *Frederick News Post*, in an article written during a heat wave in 1935, touches on the cause of the hoop snake phenomena:

> *The dog days…are upon us, and ancient role hath it that even the dew is poisoned, causing dogs to go mad and snakes to roll down hill with their tails in their mouths.*

And apparently, in the case of the snakes, to grow horns and take on magical powers of destruction. But here in wild and wonderful Western Maryland, we'd expect no less.

# A Mysterious Menagerie

If it's not one thing, it's another mysterious creature making itself known in the wilds and towns of Western Maryland. Here are a few amazing accounts of unaccountable creatures, out-of-place animals and misidentified monsters.

## Thurmont's Tapir Caper

So what was a tapir, an animal indigenous to South America and Asia, doing in Thurmont in 1971? Not very much, according to the former Frederick County magistrate, who spied it on Catoctin Hollow Road. "It was just placidly waiting for dusk," he was quoted as saying in the October 7 edition of the *Frederick News* in an article entitled "Long-Nose Tapir on the Loose." An escapee from a truck driven by the owner of a Virginia zoo, the long-nosed animal had made its getaway into a wooded area near Cunningham Falls, where it was soon spotted by alarmed locals who mistook it for everything from an armadillo to a wild boar. As with sightings of other strange creatures in the area, at least one person who reported it to the police was told to "go home and sober up." The runaway was soon properly IDed, and although the *News* likened the creature to the "mythical dwayyo" that had terrorized (or entertained) the county in the '60s, the owner of a Thurmont zoo assured residents that the tapir was harmless. At least as harmless as a three-hundred-plus-pound member of a species that's occasionally been known to maul zookeepers can be.

The *News* was prophetic in one statement made in its article. After quoting the zookeeper as saying the animal did not pose a danger, the article continued, "Frederick County, on the other hand, may be a danger to the tapir." The paper was, sadly, all too right, as the tapir met its demise at the front tire of a large pick-up truck later that month. There was, however, one caveat that's very familiar to "creature feature" fans. The *News* reported that the tapir might have given birth while on the loose in the Catoctin woods. And in the words of the final scene of almost every creature feature from the 1950s: "The End…?"

## The Dog That Went to Church

Somewhere around 1805, a hapless dog that just wanted a quiet place for a good nap inadvertently stirred up some excitement in Hagerstown. Historian Scharf described the scene:

> *Considerable excitement was created…by the announcement that the old Episcopal church was haunted. The report arose from the fact that a large black dog got into the building on Sunday and went to sleep without being observed. When he awoke the door was locked, and his howls and frantic efforts to get out alarmed the neighborhood. It is a curious evidence of the prevalence of superstition at the time that the people generally jumped to the conclusion that the church was inhabited by ghosts.*

It could also be considered curious that the historian noted that the dog couldn't get out because the door was locked, but then again, this was apparently no ordinary dog. Wrote the historian:

> *It was also gravely asserted that when the door was opened the dog sprang over the heads of twenty men.*

The dog apparently spread the word about his unfortunate experience because there have been very few church-going dogs in Hagerstown ever since.

## Man-Eating Catfish in Antietam Creek

The Mumma family knows Sharpsburg history. Not only have they lived in the area for generations, but also their family farmstead sat right smack in the middle of the Antietam battlefield. So when Wilmer Mumma wrote *Ghosts of Antietam*, a book recounting some of the legends and lore associated with the Battle of Antietam and the Sharpsburg area, you've got to figure he knew what he was talking about. And one of the most incredible tales in his book involved, not ghosts, but something quite a bit more flesh and blood.

Several months after the 1862 Battle of Antietam (notoriously known as "America's Bloodiest Day"), the small town of Sharpsburg was trying its best to get back to normal. Some of the local fellows returned to the banks of Antietam Creek to do some fishing but soon noticed something quite alarming. The catfish they were hooking seemed not only to be bigger than they used to be but also a whole lot more ornery. Fishermen at the spot known as "Molly's Hole" near the Burnside Bridge found themselves fighting to reel in catfish in much the same way that, today, we see deep sea fishermen try to reel in huge, thrashing marlins on cable TV shows. The anglers resorted to fishing with "half-inch hemp rope tied to a tree stump," but the belligerent catfish were chewing through even that.

It seemed as if the fellows of Sharpsburg had a challenging new sport on their hands, and the stouthearted fishermen were more than up to the challenge. But things soon took a turn for the ugly. A fisherman hooked one of the mutant catfish and was pulled under. When what was left of his body was recovered several days later, it was as though a great white shark had gotten hold of him; there was nothing left but a few bones and a gnawed up gold watch. It was then, said Mumma, the fishermen came to a terrible realization. A few months earlier, as casualties from the Battle of Antietam had fallen or been thrown into the water, the diet of the catfish in Antietam Creek had gotten a ghastly supplement. And not only had the fish grown unnaturally big on this horrible feast, but they also had developed a taste for human flesh. Not coincidentally, the area fishermen developed a distinct distaste for catfish, one that is said to have lasted for generations.

Before we are too quick to dismiss this as a particularly gruesome version of a "fish tale," consider this 2008 headline: "Mutant Fish Develops a Taste for Human Flesh in India." It seems people living near the Great Kali River were claiming that the local catfish population had been feeding on bodies put into the river as part of local funeral traditions just a little too long. The article recounted two incidents in which young men were pulled under water by something very big; there were witnesses to both attacks who described a large fish. If this still seems impossible, then let's consider that the largest documented catfish caught in that area a few years ago weighed in at 161 pounds and was almost six feet long.

The truth of the matter is about as murky as the waters of Antietam Creek in 1862. Although we understand some pretty big catfish are still occasionally caught in the area, we are really quite certain that they haven't feasted on human flesh. But if you are in the area and want to dine on some of the local fish, I'm going to go ahead and suggest the trout.

This image on an old postcard shows a creepy, ramshackle house in Allegany County. The caption reads, "Old Haunted House, Located on the Road built by Gen. Braddock, 1754, Cumberland, MD." We don't doubt the haunted part, but the date must be wrong. General Braddock didn't arrive in the United States until 1755. Nothing else is known about this mysterious image, except that the house may have been associated with a murder in the 1800s. *Author's collection.*

# Part 2

# Eerie Entities of Western Maryland

*No good will eber come o' talkin about ghosts.*
*—T.C. Harbaugh,* Middletown in Song and Story

The next stop on our tour of mysterious Western Maryland is a chilling one. We are about to encounter some very creepy denizens of the spirit world. But don't worry, it's not all screams and shudders. Some of the eerie entities of Western Maryland are downright playful, and some of them—well, we're not quite sure what they are—but they sure are unique. And so I give you the shadow realms of the mountainside of Maryland. And remember, there's nothing to fear but that severed hand skittering up that wall over there.

As this drawing by Washington County park ranger Mannie Gentile depicts, one never knows what he or she might encounter on a nighttime stroll in the mountains of Maryland. *Courtesy of Mannie Gentile.*

# SOUTH MOUNTAIN SPOOKS

South Mountain just may be the pinnacle of Western Maryland weirdness, and it's almost certainly home to the area's densest population of spooks. Submitted for your approval here are a few of the unearthly inhabitants of "Old South."

## *Indian Apparitions*

As you might guess, I have always loved all things spooky. So you can well imagine my shiver-down-the-spine thrill when I encountered the stories of the Indian specters of South Mountain. When Washington transplant Madeleine Dahlgren moved to South Mountain in 1882, she documented the fabulously frightening stories and legends of the area, and they are hands down some of the most unique specters I've ever come across.

The folks relating these stories to Dahlgren either seriously believed they had witnessed these apparitions or were dead serious about pulling Dahlgren's leg. Dahlgren introduced the stories by stating that the spooky tales were "by many held as facts, and [were] held as matters of serious belief." She added, "The incidents have been related to us at various times by different people, with every evidence of personal faith." Then, just to set the scene, she opened her book with some local Indian atrocity tales, complete with tomahawked children and kidnapped maidens.

It's true that South Mountain was once traversed by bands of Indians, mostly Delawares and Catawbas, who didn't particularly care for each other and showed this dislike with lots of edged weapons and bloodshed. As for the settlers, they were usually tolerated, at least until the era of the French and Indian War, at which point things took a decidedly ugly turn.

"Aunt Patty" was Dahlgren's preeminent source of phantom Indian stories, and we'll be traveling back in time with her to get introduced to some of these South Mountain Indian entities. Aunt Patty was eighty-six when she told her creepy tales to neighbor Dahlgren, and even at that advanced age, she was a force to be reckoned with. Born toward the end of the 1700s, Aunt Patty was a big gal, tough and rugged, and was, at the time, celebrated for having recently walked the five miles to the home of her younger (she was eighty-three years old) sister. It was in this sister's cozy cabin that Aunt Patty spun her yarns, and we can imagine a crackling fire casting eerie shadows, the South Mountain wind howling outside and Dahlgren leaning breathlessly forward as the old woman proclaimed that these dramatic Indian specters had once been all too plentiful: "The Injuns jist used to walk so constant like arter nite, they kep' up a kinder *procession of shades!*" (Heavy-handed patois courtesy of Ms. Dahlgren.)

But Aunt Patty and her kinfolk saw a lot more of the Indians than just this parade of spooks; as a matter of fact, they had so many encounters with these ghosts that they seemed to take them in stride, as if they were any other part of the natural landscape of South Mountain. Case in point, "whin we wuz children," she reported to Dahlgren, "we'd often's the time and agin walk one side to Middle Creek, an' the *Skiliton Injuns* jist friendly like, on t'other side, *hollerin'*; an' we wuz so used to it we didened skeer a bit."

These Indian "shades" must have been bored with the afterlife, for they seemed to seek out the company of the locals. The old mountain woman told Dahlgren of an occasion when, late one night, she and a group of friends had been strolling home from a party, following the snakelike Middle Creek through the dark woods, when they noticed "a shower of sparks" lighting up the dark path ahead. As the group got closer:

> We all sawr it was a big Injun shade with a lite in him, and the shower of sparks that wint up from him...an' he hollered fearful "Ok-en-jah!" Whin he kim to the big rock, he jist give one leap in the air, hollered "Ok-en-jah," an' wint out in the water.

While these spirits seemed generally to be of a companionable sort, one would be ill advised to annoy them. Aunt Patty's grandfather had once been joined on a late night walk by another Indian ghost with the whole lit-up-from-inside thing going on, along with the spectacular addition of flames shooting from his fingers. When the Indian "hooped an' hollered like mad" at him, the old man made a foolish move: he taunted the fearsome Indian spirit. The Indian did not have a sense of humor:

> All to wunst the Injun broke away over the stream arter gran-dad, an' he got orful skeered an' run. An' the Injun chased him clean to his door; and es granny heerd him runnin' she opened the door quick fur him, an' he jist fell inside, an' the minit the door shet, the Injun hollered orful 'Ok-en-jah!' an'

*giv a thunderin' rap on the door! As the phantom Indian pounded, the door sizzled "as ef a red-hot iron" had been thrown against it.*

This mark supposedly remained on the door until the house was torn down.

It seemed everyone who was anyone on South Mountain had an Indian ghost encounter. Aunt Patty's husband came across an "Injun spook" that was so frightening it even gave his poor pony the shakes. This Indian ghost also "had a fire in him," but it was what it didn't have—a head—that made this spook special. The locals took this startling Indian specter in stride as well, and it's no wonder: Aunt Patty said he was seen fifty times.

Even the local schoolhouse was troubled by an Indian haunting. The schoolhouse, it was said, had been built on an Indian burial ground, with the usual well-what-do-you-expect results. While the spirits didn't interfere with the students during the day, every night the building was lit up inside, from, of course, the light emanating from the flaming head of a "big Injun" ghost making himself at home inside. The schoolhouse Indian was also fond of hollering, "Ok-en-jah!"—so loudly, in this case, that it was said the mountain itself could be felt to tremble.

On another occasion, an Indian phantom actually appeared, the locals said, in the form of a large black horse, which was spied sitting in a clearing on its haunches, its front legs dangling and its glowing red eyes rolling around in its head. Noting the terror of the fellow who had the misfortune to come across it, the horse Indian spirit screamed, "Ok-en-jah!" for good measure, as the frightened guy ran down the mountain. By the way, while a translation of the phrase "Ok-en-jah" is not readily available, I am pretty sure it means something along the lines of, "Enjoy your haunted mountain, chumps."

Here in Western Maryland, we take our hats off to those pyrotechnic wizards, the Indian spirits of South Mountain. We admire their ingenuity, as well as their inclination toward being friendly to the children but messing with those who had more of a tendency to be jerks to Native Americans: the grown-ups. These Indian spooks aren't spoken of very much these days, but we like to think they are still out there, splashing through the waters of Middle Creek, shooting sparks off their fingertips and generally being really awesome.

## *Witch Margery*

She hasn't gotten nearly as much press as some other mountain spooks, maybe because the Blair Witch's PR person wouldn't return her calls or perhaps because she's just modest—although I highly doubt that. It's more likely that Witch Margery is so terrifying that they like to keep her hushed-up around these parts. After all, the young traveler who had the poor sense to visit her cabin was never heard from again, and that's not exactly good for tourism. I'll tell you his story here, based on an account given by a local writer who lived in the area over one hundred years ago, and you can make up your own mind about Witch Margery.

It was a few years before the Civil War, and a young man named Rosson Wilmot hit it off with a young traveler named Eldon George when the two happened to meet in Frederick. Rosson, a local fellow who lived near South Mountain, was a chatty sort, and as the pair rode by horseback from Frederick through Middletown and toward the mountain range, he kept Eldon entertained with a steady stream of one-sided conversation. It wasn't until they neared the mountain that he paused in his soliloquy and asked his new friend what had brought him to the area.

"Well," said Eldon, excited to at last reveal his mission, "I left Philadelphia and came here with sealed instructions from my grandfather, General Sephas George. I was not allowed to open them until I got to Frederick."

"You don't say!" exclaimed young Rosson, intrigued at this new development. "Do tell! What was in these mysterious instructions?"

"Well, inside the envelope he gave me was this little package," Eldon held up a small, well-sealed package tied up in string and continued, "and instructions to deliver it to a resident of South Mountain by the name of Margery."

"Dear God!" Rosson jerked his horse to an abrupt, dust-stirring halt and gazed with horror at the now-startled Eldon George. "*Witch* Margery?"

Eldon gave a nervous laugh at this, but something in the other man's face told him the local was not joking. Suddenly, Eldon noticed that the horses seemed jittery, and then, as if on cue, a distant rumble of thunder broke the mountain air.

"Pardon me," he said politely, "But I thought you said 'witch.'"

"I did indeed!" exclaimed the other. "Have you any idea what sort of creature it is that you are about to encounter?"

"I know nothing whatsoever of her," Eldon told his new friend. "Only that my aged grandfather said that this package must be delivered to Margery on South Mountain or he will have no peace in the next world."

"Yes, that sounds like Witch Margery, all right!" Rosson tsk-tsked. "Whatever did your grandfather get himself into? I would sooner meet Satan himself than have to face Witch Margery!"

"I guess I'm in for it then," laughed Eldon, still trying to convince himself Rosson was teasing.

"My dear boy," Rosson said excitedly, "You must understand! This old hag you've been sent to see is the Witch Queen of South Mountain. She can turn herself into any variety of creature, and they say she can even raise the dead!"

"Those sound like good tricks," Eldon said good-naturedly.

Rosson looked about anxiously. "My friend, I fear I must take my leave as they are, ah…waiting for me at home, yes, that's it!" He awkwardly pulled out a pocket watch and gave it a perfunctory glance. "I'll give you directions to Witch Margery's shack, but you must promise me you won't get too close to the old hag!"

Eldon, perplexed, gave his word, and a few moments later, he watched Rosson disappear down the road in a cloud of dust. He reined his increasingly reluctant horse toward the path his friend had directed him to just as more thunder, now much closer, seemed to shake the very mountain.

The sun was just dropping over the ridge when he finally spied a dilapidated cabin ringed by boulders and shrouded by gnarled trees ahead.

*That must be the place*, Eldon thought. "Ye gods, I can't believe the old man has business with a woman who lives in a place such as this!"

As he neared the hut, he heard what sounded like the hooting of a very irritated owl, and sure enough, Eldon spied a large owl with eyes aglow perched on the twisted limb of a tree just outside the cottage door. Just as his attention was distracted by the bird, he heard a terrible screech right behind him and turned with a panicked start.

"Just what is your business here? Speak, boy!" a voice shrieked, and from the encroaching darkness emerged a being the likes of which Eldon had never seen. Man and horse shuddered as one as they beheld a cadaverous woman who had to be, Eldon thought, at least 110 years old. The old crone was bent at the waist and cloaked in black garments over which long strands of gray hair trailed like the ragged mountain paths themselves.

Eldon dropped from the horse and tried to pretend as if he met scary old witches in the midst of thunderstorms on creepy mountains every day.

"Madam," he began, but the old woman, peering into his face, shrieked again. Eldon jumped.

"*He* sent you! I can see his blood in your face."

"I'm sure I don't…" Eldon trailed off just as a bony hand shot from inside the woman's black robes and grasped his wrist. He felt himself being pulled with unexpected might by the old hag, and in an instant, he was being led into her miserable abode. He glanced about and took in the setting with horror as he stumbled through the doorway: the worn dirt floor, a battered broomstick sitting by the fireplace, a pot of something unspeakable simmering over a fire and, in a corner, a heap of suspiciously human-looking bones.

"Maid's day off?" he offered, trying desperately to pretend it wasn't all real.

By the light of the flickering fire, he could see her plainly now. She had a multitude of wrinkles on her long, haggard face, black eyes glittering like hot coals and, worst of all, a glaring and mangy black cat perched on her round shoulder.

"I-I-I only came to bring…" Eldon stammered.

"I know what you came for. After all these years—the nerve of him! Why did the general not come himself?" the witch demanded.

Eldon glanced around the hut again. *I think I'm starting to understand why he didn't come himself*, he thought. But he said, "Well, he's getting up there you know…"

"Excuses, excuses! Well, the old man will see me soon enough," she cackled. She turned her horrible face sideways unnaturally, it seemed to Eldon, and gazed up expectantly at the poor youth, who by now had about given up on attempting to speak.

The witch extended her gnarled hand, palm upward, toward him.

"Well, what are you waiting for boy? Give it to me!" she demanded.

Eldon, trembling, produced the package from inside his coat. The bony hand snatched it from him.

"And what do you think your splendid gentleman of a grandfather has sent to me, boy?" she demanded.

"Well, it's too small to be a fruitcake…"

"Enough!" screeched Witch Margery, who had likely lost her sense of humor somewhere around the Inquisition. She tore open the small package and, to Eldon's surprise, held up between her hideously misshapen fingers a golden ring.

A bolt of lightning flashed through the hut, and the old woman screeched. "The wedding ring! After so many years, the general thinks he can make good on his promise to give me a wedding ring, does he?"

*Oh, Grannie Green is not going to like this*, Eldon was thinking just as the loudest thunderclap yet roared across the mountain, and in the next, moment everything went black and silent.

The following morning, Rosson Wilmot, plagued by a guilty conscience, rode back up the mountain at daybreak, his finger trembling on the trigger of his old rifle. What he saw when he reached Witch Margery's domicile made him gasp.

Long fingers of smoke crept up from the hut. Everything around the old shack lay blackened, surrounded by smoking trees, and a short distance away was the dead body of Eldon's poor horse. Amid all the wreckage, as still as a statue, sat a large black cat. Rosson and the cat stared at each other for only a moment before the young man slowly backed his horse away, turned it quickly and took off down the muddy road. He was sure he heard a hideous cackling right behind him until he was halfway down the mountain, and it was said the sight of the burned cabin and the thought of his lost friend haunted him until the end of his days.

Stories of witches lingered on South Mountain throughout the years, but all the locals knew to keep their distance from them. And they certainly knew better than to cross one.

Today, if you're on South Mountain and you encounter a particularly scraggly black cat—one that seems to be giving you a really grouchy stare—glance at your watch, pardon yourself and get out of Dodge ASAP, because you just might be in the presence of Witch Margery. Probably not, but hey, better safe than sorry on old South Mountain.

# A GRAVE UNDERTAKING

## *The National Museum of Civil War Medicine*

You might think working at a museum would be a quiet sort of job, but that's far from the case in Frederick, thanks to a host of ghosts that seem to be inordinately fond of this local museum. Maybe it's the relics. Maybe it's the fact that the museum is in such a historic building. Or maybe ghosts just have a supernatural attraction to docents and "Do Not Touch" signs. You should visit Frederick and check out this great museum for yourself. But for now, get cozy on your couch and join this special ghost tour of the National Museum of Civil War Medicine. Tipping is appreciated.

The ghosts in this downtown Frederick museum are often playful, but sometimes they're downright scary. And it's no wonder. The building was used not only for undertaking for many years but also, at one point, by a doctor who became notorious for both a macabre Civil War photo he posed for and some very unsavory practices he supposedly engaged in. Embalming and unsavory practices don't exactly make a recipe for good karma.

Back in the 1800s, furniture making and undertaking went hand-in-hand (because there's no one better to make your mother-in-law's casket than the guy who made your kitchen table). A fellow named James Whitehill ran the undertaking and furniture-making endeavor in the building that now houses the museum from the 1830s until after the Civil War. With the War Between the States came many sadly necessary breakthroughs in the field of undertaking, most notably the rise of embalming. Sometime after the war, a Mr. Clarence Carty took over Whitehill's business. But it just may be another man, one who moonlighted there during the fall of 1862, who is responsible for the unhappy spirits who now inhabit the museum.

Dr. Richard Burr is known for several things. He is often credited with pioneering the arterial embalming process. Arterial embalming, by the way (you might want to put down that sandwich), is the process of commandeering the body's vascular system to drain out the blood while pumping the body full of those helpful chemicals better known as embalming fluid. Burr is also the guy shown embalming an unnamed soldier who is stretched out on a weathered door in the famous and chilling Matthew Brady photo. Yes, somebody had to do it—but nobody had to do the other things Dr. Burr has been accused of doing—namely, robbing the bodies of the dead and dying on the battlefields and, in his spare time, selling and reselling the same headstone over and over again. Like a ravenous buzzard, Burr hovered over the battlefields of the Civil War, waiting for the opportunity to ply his trade and perhaps pick up a little something extra by rummaging through the pockets and knapsacks of the casualties of war.

Burr was a general physician before the war, but after enlisting, he found his niche as an embalming surgeon. In September 1862 fate smiled a ghoulish smile on Burr in the form of the Battles of South Mountain and Antietam. The enterprising embalmer was soon encamped in the conveniently located undertaking establishment of Mr. Whitehill, ready to swoop in as scores of bodies piled up. So perhaps it was the long-ago presence of the nefarious Dr. Burr that put the spirits of 48 East Patrick in such a bad mood. Whatever it was, there have long been tales

Dr. Richard Burr, who plied his trade in the building that now houses the National Museum of Civil War Medicine in Frederick, is shown embalming an unknown soldier during the Civil War. *Library of Congress.*

of ghosts associated with the building, and many of the descriptions of the spirits spotted in the museum involve the words "angry" and "not happy looking."

Perhaps the most striking spirit seen in the National Museum of Civil War Medicine is the one often called John Hardt, who is said to have been a one-time employee of the undertaking business. As if it wouldn't be alarming enough to encounter a ghost, this spirit is described as grim faced, imposingly tall and sporting high black boots. At least one person has reported being punched by this intimidating ghost. The foul-tempered fellow has also been alternatively identified as both Carty and Whitehill; but then again, perhaps he is the disgruntled spirit of one of those unfortunate men the greedy Dr. Burr embalmed and possibly robbed in the bloody days of 1862.

Another frequently seen specter is known as the Woman in Gray. Sporting clothing from the 1800s and a sour expression, the Woman in Gray has been spotted again and again over the years. "I walked into her coming out of the bathroom," a female employee reported recently. "She was not happy." On another occasion, a sighting of the Woman in Gray is said to have sent a tutor, who was working with a staff member's daughter in the third-floor research library, running out the front door.

Not all of the ghosts are quite so menacing. As a matter of fact, some of them are what passes as playful in the spirit world. Paperclips inexplicably shooting out of their holders in staff offices, books flying off shelves in the museum bookstore, the laughter of children, an invisible somebody ringing the doorbell—these things have happened so many times the museum staff members hardly bat their eyes. They say that the spirited ghosts seem to be especially fond of the ramps that separate the floors of the museum, and visitors shouldn't be surprised to hear the pitter patter of phantom footsteps behind them. A ghostly figure wearing a large straw hat was once seen strolling up a ramp by a worker watching a security monitor. And the spirits might not all be human; the museum's director occasionally hears a phantom kitty clawing on the carpet in his office.

If you visit the National Museum of Civil War Medicine, you can say, "Howdy" to the infamous Dr. Burr. There is a very striking, life-size tableau of the Matthew Brady photo of Burr in action on display. In creepy mannequin form, he is captured eternally in the unsettling act of embalming an unfortunate soldier.

Oh, and by the way, on your way out, if a book flies off the shelf at you in the museum bookstore, take it as a well-meant suggestion: buy the book.

# A Study in Spirits

## Mount Saint Mary's University

The college experience: late nights spent cramming for exams, parties, new friends, disembodied hands, the ghost of the Drunken Nun, the bruises on your body from having objects thrown at you by angry ghosts…

Wait—what? Yes, these and other chilling experiences may await those fortunate enough to attend Mount Saint Mary's University in

This photograph was taken at Mount Saint Mary's in Emmitsburg during the Battle of Gettysburg. *Library of Congress.*

Emmitsburg. The picturesque seminary and liberal arts college boasts a cozy, nestled-in-the-mountains locale, a world-renowned theological program and a fourteen-to-one student-to-faculty ratio. It's also home to some of the most notorious, varied and, best of all, active spirits ever heard of. The fourteen-to-one ratio could also be the student-to-ghost ratio. The campus is practically crawling with spirits.

It's little wonder Mount Saint Mary's is infested with ghosts. Founded in 1808, the Mount, as it's called, has over two hundred years of history—history that encompasses slavery, war and religious fervor. Central to the otherworldly goings-on at the Mount are a host of characters (and parts of characters) that once called the campus home. Let's take a little tour and find out more about them. You might want to walk a little faster—the sun is setting behind the Catoctin Mountains, and strange shadows are beginning to loom against the stone façade of the university's old chapel.

We should warn you that, as we stroll across the campus, you might feel a gentle but firm tap on your shoulder. This is probably just the Ghost Soldier. Don't worry, he's a campus regular who has only one request: "Please, roll me over." You see, this unfortunate soul is the spirit of a man who was wounded in the 1863 Battle of Gettysburg and made it as far as Emmitsburg before succumbing to his wounds. According to the story, the soldier had parted from his sweetheart before the war with a charming sentiment involving "gazing at the same sky for all of eternity," meaning in the event he got killed in the war, his beloved should take comfort in knowing that they would be gazing at the same sky for all eternity—from the comfort of their graves, that is. A nice piece of jewelry to remember him by might have been a nicer parting gift. Unfortunately, this lovers' pact, like so many are, was destined to be broken. A careless gravedigger put our hero into the grave on his stomach. Ever since, the fretful spirit of the soldier has roamed the campus, eternally requesting to have his mortal remains rolled over so that he and the little lady (wherever she ended up being buried) can commence with that their gazing.

Let's duck inside a few minutes—it's getting a little spooky out here. Way to go, you've chosen to take shelter in the Terrace Dorm. You're about to find out how haunted it is in here. Sure, the ghost of the Drunken Nun sounds fun, but apparently, she's a mean drunk. The soused sister met her end one snowy night when she stepped out onto the icy steps after having a few too many. Ever since, she's had an unfortunate tendency to trash dorm rooms like a jilted girlfriend with anger management issues. Her most annoying ghostly superpower is the ability to cause electrical outages, much to the consternation of students who find it challenging to study in the dark with no Internet access. It is said, however, that she can be appeased by leaving an open can of beer sitting out for her, so just to be safe, let's pop open that Natty Boh and leave it on the table while we head upstairs.

Don't worry, we're not going to see another ghost, at least not yet. We're just paying a quick visit to a little room alluringly named "the Bleeding Room." Actually two rooms, one of them now a janitor's closet, they are famous for the red sticky substance that seems to ooze right through the walls. Although no explanation has ever been found, workers have tried time and again to fix the problem, but the mysterious "blood" always returns.

Since we might be starting to feel a bit woozy, let's step back outside for some fresh air. And let's hope if we encounter another spirit out on the now darkened quad, it's that of Father Dubois. As the founder of the Mount, Dubois is not only among the highest ranking in the paranormal pantheon on campus but also a kind-hearted ghost if ever there was one. Apparently every now and then, a student with a troubled heart will stop to sit on the lawn in front of the seminary building to ruminate about his troubles, only to have the comforting figure of the old priest suddenly appear. This off-the-clock therapist will listen to the student's woes and sometimes even offer tidbits of wisdom before disappearing.

Bishop Simon Brute, one of the founding fathers of Mount Saint Mary's University, is shown in this undated drawing. *Courtesy of Mount Saint Mary's University, Phillips Library.*

Joining Father Dubois as the other half of the campus's haunted homecoming couple is the ghost of Elizabeth Ann Seton, or Mother Seton, as she is known. Mother Seton is remembered as an all-around good soul who founded a religious community in the area specifically to help impoverished children. To this day, she is occasionally spotted strolling the campus in spirit form, sporting a demure cloak and bonnet and carrying a rosary and Bible. Sometimes, she's accompanied by an unidentified ghostly male companion, but that's no business of ours.

Before we get too cozy out here, I should warn you about the entity known as "the Hand" because, really, it could appear at any time while we're out here on the Terrace Quad, and the tale of the Hand is kind of disturbing. You see, part of the darker history of the campus is that, once upon a time, as one of history's little (okay, big) ironies, slaves were held at the seminary. One of these unfortunate souls, a slave named Leander, was accused of stealing (which probably involved something along the lines of what we refer to nowadays as "having dinner"). As punishment, Leander's hand was cut off and, it is said, buried somewhere in the quad. Ever since, the disembodied hand has been skittering around the campus, crawling up the side of a building here and scratching at a window there. It has also long been maintained that one can hear Leander's screams echoing across the campus on particularly still, creepy nights, such as tonight. What's that? You'd like to go back inside? Fantastic—we know just the place.

It's the epicenter of Mount Saint Mary's paranormal shenanigans. Known as Brute 252 in the Terrace Dorm, it's a room so haunted that it actually sat empty for many years. And we are about to get the real low-down on the notorious Brute 252 because, as luck would have it, we have a special guest tour guide: 2011 Mount Saint Mary's graduate Jake Yohn. Jake, along with several roommates, lived in Brute 252. If you've ever wondered what it would be like to live in a haunted dorm, it seems it's really kind of a pain in the neck more than anything. Expect to make a lot of calls to maintenance about weird problems with your electricity. Plan to do a lot of cleaning up of broken objects, toppled furniture and emptied-out drawers. Count on being startled by apparitions that appear when you least expect it. And don't get too relaxed while you're sitting there watching TV or working on your term paper because you never know when books will suddenly fly off shelves or the door to the room will fling itself open dramatically. And much like the upperclassmen in every teen movie you've ever seen, these spirits seem to like to pick on freshmen. Jake says many of his supernatural experiences occurred during his freshman year. It was in the Terrace Dorm that Jake actually saw the Mount's most daunting ghost: Reverend Simon Brute.

While there is nothing dark or scandalous in Reverend Brute's history, his ghost is often described as "gruff looking" and seems to provoke a sense of fear and intimidation in students. Gaunt faced and clad in flowing black robes, Reverend Brute is usually seen wandering the hallways, which is where Jake ran into him:

*I personally saw Reverend Brute wandering the halls at least twice. My first encounter, he nodded politely and moved on...When I realized seconds later who he was, I spun around, but he was gone. It spooked me pretty bad, and I had to be coaxed out of the room later for dinner. The second time I saw him it was several months later, and we were fairly used to his antics. I openly acknowledged him, but he ignored me and continued walking on.*

As if being snubbed by Reverend Brute wasn't bad enough, Jake and his roommates had to endure their TV changing channels on its own, books flying across the room and paranormal cold spots. And while we can't say for sure that the austere Reverend Brute was to blame, one of the ghosts in the dorm seemed to get kind of aggressive when a classmate of Jake's lit up something not strictly legal in 252. The toker was alone in the room when a metal fan flew across the dorm as if hurled by an unseen and somewhat judgmental hand. It struck him in the stomach, leaving some nasty bruises.

Now that we've experienced the after-hours tour of haunted Mount Saint Mary's, we'll move on and leave the students to their studying and their spirits; that fourteen-to-one student-to-ghost ratio seems to suit them just fine. Despite the scares and the destructive hijinks, the Mount embraces its ghosts, and the upperclassmen appreciate the fact that they don't have to waste their time harassing freshmen: the spirits have got that covered.

# HAGERSTOWN HAUNTS

Dave Dull is a very ironically named fellow. As a producer for Antietam Cable in Hagerstown, he has had plenty of adventures while creating numerous series on local history. In one of these programs, *Legends of Washington County*, Dave and his crew documented some of the many weird tales associated with the area. The stories about Haunted Hagerstown are some of the most intriguing, so we're going to follow in Dave's footsteps and check out two of these great spots:

## *Hager House Haunts Torment Tour Guides*

The Hager House was built in 1739 by Jonathan Hager, the gentleman who is often called Hagerstown's founding father. It was a home, but it was also designed to serve as a sort of self-contained fort: thick stone walls offered protection from arrows and bullets, narrow openings in the walls provided relatively safe places to fire back at attackers and the stream flowing through the basement created an indoor water source. The house served as a residence to many families over the course of the following two hundred years. Today, standing in the midst of the Hagerstown City Park, it looks much the same as it did in its early years—right down to the presence of some of its former occupants, who apparently have a disconcerting tendency to show up now and then. Tour guides at the Hager House have long had to put up with these troublesome "co-workers," who seem to spend an awful lot of the workday trying to get attention.

If you are interested in becoming a tour guide at the Hager House, here are a few qualifications that could be on the job description:

Inside the Hager House, accoutrements of surviving in Ye Olde Western Maryland are on display, including big guns, warm animal skins and lots of blunt objects. *Author's photo.*

- Ability to withstand being poked by unseen fingers.
- Tolerance for being a source of mirth for unseen gigglers.
- Willingness to put up with very unpredictable phantom smells. (Just when the delicious smell of that invisible cherry pie starts making your mouth water, it may be replaced by the pungent smell of pipe tobacco.)
- Love for mischievous children, especially invisible ones.
- Patience with inanimate objects that move by themselves.
- Capability to deal with unexpected appearances of spirits while leading tours.

John Bryan is in a position to answer just how haunted the Hager House really is. The local historian spent at least twelve years working at the Hager House, and he says there's actually a perfectly good reason why there really could be ghosts there: "We know thirteen people died in the house."

Most of the people who died in the Hager House weren't Hagers but other folks who called the house home during the 1800s. While they seem to be having a bit of fun with the place now, in the 1800s, the Hager House was a hard-luck place for these unfortunates. In one family alone, both parents and five of their children perished inside.

But these spirits are good sports. Despite their tragic endings, they seem to have found their niche as paranormal pranksters and enjoy teasing the tour guides. Much of the activity in the house—such as the sounds of footsteps running up the stairs, a corncob doll that just won't stay in one place and disembodied laughter—have been attributed to the ghost children.

The Hager House spirits show themselves on occasion as well. A guide giving a tour was once startled by the ghost of a young woman in green passing through the room, and a ghostly man is sometimes spotted enjoying a pipe on the front porch.

It's not all fun, games and relaxation at the Hager House, however. The basement seems to have especially creepy mojo, and it was while filming a tour video there that Dave Dull and his crew ran into some unexpected technical difficulties. According to Dave:

*We were setting up in the basement, and our portable audio mixer just stopped working. It literally died. We changed batteries, and that didn't work. So we had to stop. We shipped the unit out for repair to the manufacturer. They ended up sending us a new one because they couldn't figure out why it had stopped working.*

John Bryan once found himself the subject of some very determined prodding while heading upstairs to retrieve a shirt from a bedroom during a photo shoot in the house:

*I felt what I can only describe as a "poke in the back"; it was strange, the feeling of coldness and like that spot went to sleep, only a moment, but startling. I went on up to the bedroom and bent over to retrieve the shirt... and felt another poke, so I figured someone didn't want me to use that, so I went and got something else.*

Entity enthusiasts might point out that some of the activity in the Hager House could be facilitated by the fact that it's built of fieldstone over two springs; water and stone are both considered powerful paranormal conduits. Ghosts or not, the Hager House offers visitors an evocative glimpse into the lives of early Western Marylanders.

## The Ghost in the Town Square

Take an evening stroll through Hagerstown's town square on any July 6, and you just might get the feeling you're being watched from above. Then, just as this eerie feeling causes your eyes travel to the top of the building often called the "clock tower," you jump as agonized screams shriek across the darkness.

Don't run for your car—it's all perfectly natural in downtown Haunted Hagerstown. Or it's at least what can you expect when a young artist takes a bullet to the head atop what is now the location of the town's most recognizable building.

As documented by Dave Dull and crew, John Stemple was an ambitious local artist who apparently had a what-was-he-thinking moment in July 1863 as Judson Kilpatrick's cavalry chased Confederate regiments retreating from Gettysburg through the streets of Hagerstown. It must have been an incredibly dramatic scene: horses thundering through the streets of the city, cavalry exchanging shots, bystanders running for shelter. Perhaps it's understandable that an artist would want to capture that moment in history. Unfortunately, placing himself in the middle of the action while he set up an easel and tripod was probably not a particularly wise move, and poor Stemple quickly caught a stray bullet in the head. The bleeding man was carried down from the roof and across the square to the home of a woman who "practiced medicine," but within an hour, John Stemple was dead.

Today, the clock tower building stands in the spot once occupied by the store on top of which Stemple began his last drawing. Folks swear that each year on the anniversary of the Battle of Hagerstown, cries of pain can be heard emanating from the rooftop area. They also say that sometimes the ghostly figure of a man believed to be Stemple can be seen staring down from one of the windows of the building, perhaps watching a phantom battle play out below in the streets of Hagerstown.

## Assorted Entities

And a few more strange beings of note can be found in Allegany County, Williamsport, Cumberland and Deep Creek Lake.

### *Little Green Men*

Okay, so they're not exactly eerie—unless you've seen certain horror movies from the '90s, anyway. But still, you might not expect the mountains of Allegany County, Maryland, to be infested with those top hat–wearing wee hoarders known as leprechauns.

The Allegany leprechauns make their presence known mainly via the small lights they are said to carry as they go about their leprechaun business in the dark of the Western Maryland night. These lights have been spotted since the 1700s, flickering mysteriously in the hills outside Cumberland. The story of how the leprechauns got so far from their ancestral home and just what they've been up to in the mountains is, as you might imagine, an interesting one.

It all started with a certain British officer, General Edward Braddock, who came to America in 1755 to take on those party-crashing French who had been all too busy sweet-talking Indians and generally stirring up trouble for the colonists. In addition to his American expedition not going too well on the military front, it seems we can thank Braddock for the leprechaun invasion.

You see, General Braddock left for America from Ireland. Apparently, a group of leprechauns were dissatisfied with the pot-of-gold situation in Cork, and, I'm assuming, they also anticipated the creation of a certain American breakfast cereal full of marshmallow goodness. So they did what any restless leprechauns would do: hitched a ride on Braddock's ship in search of magical adventures. Braddock and his army eventually wound up in Western Maryland at Fort Cumberland, and according to legend, when they left the fort for Philadelphia, they hid a large amount of gold somewhere in the local mountains. The leprechauns, who had been aware of the cache of cash Braddock had been transporting, had followed the army into the Maryland mountains, and when the gold stayed, they stayed. Navigation wasn't Braddock's men's strong suit, and the army was never able to recover its hidden gold. Since the 1700s, many treasure hunters have searched for the lost stash, but it has never been found.

They are rarely sighted and aren't very cooperative at census time, but it's safe to say that the lantern-carrying leprechauns are established and industrious residents of Allegany County.

## *Weird in Williamsport*

In 1900, the *Hagerstown Mail* reported two strange stories of bizarre sightings: one of an entity that had something it shouldn't and the other of an entity that seemed to be missing something.

It was nothing less than a headless ghost that had residents of Williamsport, the lovely little town along the C&O Canal, alarmed during the winter of 1900. And according to the *Mail*, the information came from a "very reliable source," so, you know, that's good enough for us. According to this reliable source, the "blood-curdling" sight was witnessed nearly every night for several weeks. The unsettling apparition was first sighted along the canal at Two Banks by a pair of young men who ran home in terror. Soon, numerous people in the area were having their own encounters. The ghost, who carried a lighted lantern, gave the appearance of being a real person, except that it was minus a head. The headless one caused quite a scare, as the *Mail* reported, "The superstitious people of the country around are living in a state of awe and terror and will not venture out at night for fear of encountering the apparition."

The headless ghost wasn't the only strange being sighted in Williamsport that year. In August, readers of the *Mail* must have given a collective gasp when they spied an article with the heading "Saw Strange Sight: Adventure of Mr. Hindshaw Near Williamsport. Was It the Bearded Lady? Stops at a House for a Drink, and Encounters a Strange Being." According to the article, a geology student from Johns Hopkins was on a rock-collecting expedition when he came upon a "colonial mansion" near Williamsport. He approached, planning to knock on the door and ask for a glass of water, despite the fact that something seemed not quite hospitable about the shuttered home. I'll let the *Mail* describe what happened next:

> *Suddenly Mr. Hindshaw says, he was aware that a human being had appeared on the scene, but whether a man or woman he was at a loss to determine. Up and down the veranda walked the strange creature, clothed in a whitish-grey skirt and shirt waist and a kitchen apron. The feet were bare, and the head with its short hair was that of a handsome man of 35. A well-grown beard added to the incongruity.*

Mr. Hindshaw was apparently very thirsty because although he thought the person on the veranda was strange enough to be reported to the newspaper, the geologist nonetheless approached and asked for a drink. That's when

> *the man, if it is a man…looked somewhat dreamingly at Hindshaw and, turning, walked the length of the porch without a word. The strange creature came back, stopped, and looked loftily but without curiosity… when the request for a glass of water was repeated, [it] turned again and walked away.*

And the moral of that is to always carry lots of water (in a stainless steel bottle, not a plastic one, of course) and, when visiting Williamsport, always mind your own business.

## The Veiled Lady of Cumberland

According to the *Cumberland Times*, an apparition known as "the Veiled Lady" was a regular visitor to that city in the late 1800s and early 1900s.

Shrouded in black garments and, obviously, wearing a veil, she seemed to be fond of hanging out on Maryland Avenue and South Mechanic Street. The *Times* reported that the phantom had been especially busy in 1897:

> The "veiled lady" was once again a source of much discussion in the city. This supposed shadowy figure had been reported as loitering and peeping on South Mechanic Street. Small children were afraid to go on the street at night.

It was probably just as well that small children weren't running the streets of Cumberland at night. And as for the ghost, with all those misdemeanors on her rap sheet, it's no wonder she wore a veil.

## Carmel Cove Monks

The Carmelite Friars were a hardy bunch. The order began in the twelfth century with a community of hermits in Israel, and when they purchased fifty-three acres of land in Western Maryland near Deep Creek Lake in 1945, they got right to work building themselves a Western Maryland monastery. And I mean literally building it—by hand. So perhaps that's why the Carmelite Friars are still so attached to the monastery at which, to this day, they will occasionally make their presence known, though it is now the Carmel Cove Inn Bed and Breakfast.

The monastery built by the friars was a simple one: ten small rooms called cells, a community room with a small kitchen and what they called an "open bathing area." Had we been there, we would have been praying for a mild winter, because the monastery had neither heat nor a fireplace. By the 1980s, the monastery had fallen into disuse; it was purchased by a developer, and the property was subdivided into vacation properties. But the developer, perhaps sensing the presence of monks past, was "too superstitious" to tear down the old monastery and its chapel, and instead sold it to its current owner, who incorporated the monastery into a charming bed-and-breakfast.

Today, the owner of the Carmel Cove Inn Bed and Breakfast says that visitors will sometimes report "feeling a presence" and hearing odd noises. But the most striking evidence that some of the monks have perhaps stayed at Carmel Cove—in spirit anyway—came to light when the owner came across some of the friars' old blueprints of the monastery and decided to have them framed for display. It was only after hanging one of the blueprints that she saw what she says is an unmistakable face with an ecclesiastical headdress on, eerily visible if you look at the blueprint from just the right angle.

These days, if you stay at the bed-and-breakfast, you can check it out for yourself. The blueprint is hanging in the chapel, the wizened old face of a monk staring out, quite possibly judging you for enjoying that complimentary Wi-Fi, the cable television, the crackling fireplace and, especially, that luxurious private bath.

# Part 3

# Western Maryland Weird Hall of Fame

*The fun fever began to rise high…*
—Forty-four Years in the Life of a Hunter,
*Meshach Browning*

A trip to weird and wonderful Western Maryland wouldn't be complete if we didn't pause to recognize a sampling of some of the very special people who have done their share to make the area the unique place it is. From building perplexing compounds and monuments to casting magic spells and conquering the frontier one blood-soaked brawl at a time, these guys showed that being a character could be a good thing. And so, friends, I give you the Western Maryland Weird Hall of Fame. Clothing is optional.

## GEORGE ALFRED TOWNSEND

### *A Man, a Mountain and a Mausoleum*

Hold on tight, fellow travelers, we are about to ascend South Mountain to pay a visit to the one-of-a-kind locale that is Gathland State Park. You may be a bit startled when we crest the hilltop at Crampton's Gap and the eerie landscape of Gapland comes into view.

Gapland is shown in its heyday with the Civil War Correspondents' Memorial Arch in the foreground in this vintage postcard image. *Author's collection.*

The first thing you see will be the grim stone structure known as the War Correspondents' Memorial Arch, which looms ominously over the terrain. Next, you might notice the crumbling ruins of a strange old building off in a field to our left while on the right stand several old stone houses, a random stone arch and a mausoleum, moldering and haunting, replete with iron bars.

As if all this weren't disconcerting enough, there's the fact that a bloody Civil War battle once raged on this very property.

For an added touch, as we follow the road through Gapland—down one of those stretches known as "Spook Hill" no less, where helpful ghosts of Civil War soldiers will supposedly swarm your car like pesky window washers—we will quickly reach the little town of Burkittsville, the city of *Blair Witch Project* fame.

When George Alfred Townsend—better known simply as "Gath"—bought the property and commenced building his compound in 1884, weirdness was the last thing on his mind. This was the realization of a dream, albeit one some folks consider a wee bit strange, for the then well-known writer.

Gath was born in 1841 in Delaware to a circuit-rider preacher and his wife. His childhood was trying; the family was poor, and the boy seemed to have a knack for being on hand to witness executions. A typical childhood memory included the time a friend, the son of a jailor, pushed him inside a cell, locking him in with a group of bloodthirsty murderers. But young Gath was ambitious. He found his calling early and started writing; soon he

George Alfred Townsend—better known simply as "Gath"— hobnobbed with fellow writers Mark Twain and David Gray in this undated photo. *Library of Congress.*

was editing big-city newspapers. In 1861, he became one of the youngest of the Civil War correspondents (he's often called "the youngest" of the war correspondents, but this is likely not true). After the war, his newspaper columns made him a household name, and the prolific writer was said to be researching a novel when his travels brought him to the mountaintop property he would buy and christen Gapland for the mountain gap in which it lay. Always a man ahead of his time, Gath, who worked out of Washington, D.C., intended to build a sort of commuter home, and the rotund, well-dressed gentleman settled in with wife Bessie and their two children. Soon, one thing led to another, and the quiet landscape began to be transformed into a most unique compound.

Starting with a building he named (yes, he named all of his buildings) Askalon, the energetic Gath had a new hobby on his hands: architecture. Over the coming years, he designed quite a few buildings for his unusual estate (at least nine or ten), and since he had a thing for archways, stone and dramatic flourishes, the property took on a gothic look. Gath planted an orchard of one thousand trees and enclosed the estate in three thousand feet of stone fence. But it was arguably the mausoleum—intended to keep the family together for the long haul—that became the *pièce de résistance* of the compound. A bronze dog guarded the tomb from the roof, marble embellished the entrance and the words "Good Night Gath" soothingly waited to welcome the crypt's designer. None of this seemed macabre to Gath at the time; as a matter of fact, there is a photo, taken during Gath's residence at Gapland, showing unknown persons—perhaps his family— posing at the mausoleum like happy picnickers.

But locals, many of them farmers, considered the estate absurdly baronial and Gath something of a pompous jerk. You could say they just didn't get him. Gath didn't do much to help his reputation with the townies when he and some associates decided to implement a toll on the road that went through Gapland, a road commonly used by the farmers in their daily activities. Perhaps his impoverished upbringing made him overly zealous where money was involved. But the busy journalist carried on with his idiosyncratic estate building, all the while churning out scads of articles, poems and novels in the dwelling he called "the Den and Library" while his wife did, well, whatever it was she did in her own building elsewhere on the property.

Author and Frederick County native Thomas Harbaugh visited Gapland during its heyday and recounted tales of "bon vivant" Gath entertaining "the nation's great men." He described Gath's wife, Bessie, as "an accomplished and beautiful woman who knew how to pass the wine to her husband's guests and to empty as many flowing bowls as the most thirsty visitor." In other words, the girl could party with the best of them.

Harbaugh described Gapland as full of mirth, art and books. He concluded that Gath was a brilliant man who tried to re-create in his rustic home the places his active intellect secretly yearned for: the great cities of Europe.

While the "happy ending" of Gath's story was supposed to go that Gapland would be handed down to Townsend progeny while Gath and his wife slumbered contentedly in the tomb nearby, life is a tale even the best author can't script.

When George Alfred Townsend had his own personal mausoleum built next to his home at what was then known as Gapland, he intended to rest there for eternity. Sadly, although Townsend passed away a century ago, the tomb remains empty. *Author's photo.*

One of George Alfred Townsend's beloved buildings is captured forever in a sad state of disrepair in this 1920 photograph. *Library of Congress.*

When Bessie passed away, at the request of her extended family, she was buried not in the tomb at Gapland but in a family plot in Philadelphia. As Gath aged and poor health set in, he left his beloved estate to be nursed by his daughter in New York City, where he died in 1914. It only made sense for his daughter to bury him next to his wife in Philadelphia. The waiting tomb at Gapland was destined to remain empty.

At the time of his death, Gath was seemingly estranged from his son, and his daughter had married well and was living a comfortable life in New York. No one—save the locals who ransacked the compound after his death, even stealing the bronze dog from Gath's crypt—seemed to care about the estate. The era of Gapland seemed to be over.

George Alfred Townsend, it turns out, may have been more of a visionary than just the weird compound–building type he is often dismissed as being. Several years before his death, the master of the estate commissioned the

A cut-out figure of an eternally jovial George Alfred Townsend greets visitors to the museum in his honor at Gathland State Park. *Author's photo.*

building of another curious stone structure at Gapland, and this one was a doozy: the Civil War Correspondents' Memorial Arch. It is this monument that has ensured that Gath and Gapland (renamed "Gathland" when it was taken over by the State of Maryland) live on. Thanks to Gath and his desire to leave a legacy, the often-overlooked correspondents and artists of the Civil War are memorialized forever on the craggy mountaintop where the writer once ruled.

And in keeping with that empty tomb, there are whisperings that maybe Gath hasn't left his estate after all. When recent renovations were underway at Gathland's visitor center—the building named Gathland Hall by Gath—workers were pestered by knocks on doors and windows. When they would peer out, all they would see was the breeze bending the trees over the ruins of Gath's wonderland and the strange, arched monument in the distance, waiting to welcome visitors and to tell its dramatic tale.

## FISTFIGHTS WITH WOLVES

### *Meshach Browning, Western Maryland's Celebrated Hunter*

Today, the words "hunting trip" commonly evoke images of gearing up in the new Cabela's jacket and boots you got for Christmas, stowing a cooler of refreshments in a pickup and heading out to a well-appointed tree stand. Next comes a nice clean gunshot from your new hunting rifle, followed by a quick field dressing and then it's off to the processor, where you return a few days later to pick up your freezer-ready venison.

Now travel back in time with me to the year 1815. We're going to take a little hunting trip with Western Maryland's legendary huntsman, Meshach Browning. First you're going to want to whistle for your faithful hunting dog, the one with the missing eye from that little incident on the last hunting trip. Oh, and you can carry that gun if you want, but there's a pretty good chance the fatal blow to the bear, or panther or large and angry buck is going to be delivered with a knife. So don't worry too much about what you wear; you will get blood on it. And if it seems like your clothing might in any way interfere with your hunting—and believe me, it will—be prepared to dispense with it altogether. We just might get naked out in the wilderness while carrying sharp objects. And speaking of that knife, once your prey is dead you're going to be using it to cut open its stomach so you can poke

Meshach Browning, Garrett County's famed hunter. He is credited with killing an astounding number of animals, many of them without using a firearm. *From* Forty-four Years in the Life of a Hunter.

around to get a good look at the contents; that's the best way to find out what the critter's been eating, which will give us a clue as to the best place to hunt for more critters.

It may sound a little hardcore, but it seemed to work pretty well for Meshach Browning. The Garrett County outdoorsman is credited with bagging close to two thousand deer, three or four hundred bear, fifty panthers and catamounts and "scores" of wolves. And he documented it all in his memoir (said to be written with a turkey quill), *Forty-four Years in the Life of a Hunter*, published in 1859.

You can hardly fault Meshach for being unrefined. To call his childhood hardscrabble would be like saying people in Maryland think the Baltimore Ravens are okay. Meshach was born on a small farm in Frederick County in 1781, and within two weeks of his birth, his father was dead. His mother, left with no means to support her four children, gave Meshach's brother Jeremiah away to another family. There must have been a spark of adventure in Mrs. Browning, however, for it wasn't long before she decided to load a rickety wagon with her remaining kids and head for the "backwoods," or Western Maryland, where she had friends. But fortune once again frowned on the hapless Brownings. Their wagon tumbled off the road on Western Maryland's notoriously treacherous Sideling Hill, at a spot with a "considerable precipice," and little Meshach was thrown from the wagon. He was found "stunned, breathless, mangled and black with suffocation." In his book, Browning notes that the whole situation—the smashed wagon, the ruined possessions and the critically injured baby—left the widow "in low spirits."

The plucky Brownings bounced back once more, however, and the family settled into a patched-together house on twenty acres in Allegany County. But fate had another Dickens-meets-the-Alleghenies twist in store for young Meshach. A neighboring aunt and uncle he was staying with decided to steal away farther west—and took the boy with them. He would not live with his mother and siblings again.

Little Meshach was a glass-half-full kind of frontier kid, though, and he did like one thing about his new home in the Blooming Rose area of what would become Garrett County: the mountains teeming with wildlife. "Here we were in the place I had so long been looking for…the country abounded with deer, bears, panthers, wolves, wild cats, catamounts, wild turkeys, foxes, rabbits, pheasants, partridges, wild bees, and in all the streams trout without number." Perhaps it was an innate love of the outdoors, or maybe it was the fact that his aunt "had long been in the habit of flogging [him] very severely," but Meshach seemed to feel most at home out in nature.

In 1799, the eighteen-year-old Meshach married his longtime flame, Mary, and a few days after the wedding, his new father-in-law flung open their bedroom door and growled, "Rise up, sir, and go to work at something to maintain your wife!" The honeymoon was over, and it would soon become apparent that Meshach's "work" would be hunting.

It was through hunting that Meshach's individuality came out. His technique was hands-on bordering on primitive; as a matter of fact, the muscular, six-foot-one Meshach often got into fistfights with members of the animal kingdom. It was no wonder he often used the expression "getting into a fight with" instead of "hunting." And, as Meshach liked to say, "the harder the fight the better I like the fun." Here's part of his account of a tussle with a bear:

> *I stood till he came within reach when I struck him in the ear as hard as I could, and turned his head round. He made another sudden attempt to run under at my legs, when, seeing that he would get hold of me if I stood still, I made a leap, and, as he came on, landed in his rear.*

This UFC-style brawling went on for a while until "the contest becoming close," and his hunting dogs, which were always pitching in with a well-placed bite to the throat, grew weary. Then, the mountain man resorted to using his knife "and with one stab put an end to the fight." On another occasion, Meshach fought a buck in a raging stream, grabbing hold of its antlers and half drowning the huge animal before finally cutting its throat. Meshach, by the way, often seemed to find himself "fighting" deer in the water and was prepared to dispense with any unnecessary clothing at the drop of a hat. "The less clothes we had on the better," he commented.

It wasn't just his technique that was remarkable but also the sheer volume of animals Meshach bagged, as indicated by this comment in his memoir: "My spoils that morning were three bears, and a magnificent buck, all fat, cleanly handled, and taken in a very short time; for, at a little after nine o'clock I was at home, eating my breakfast."

Meshach's hunting was no mere gratuitous bloodbath. While it's undeniable he enjoyed it (you might call it bloodlust; Meshach called it "the fun fever"), it was also the way he fed and supported his family as well as kept them safe—in the wilds of Western Maryland, killing was sometimes a matter of them or us. Case in point, hungry bears were known to invade hog pens, making themselves at home while feasting one slow bite at a time on still living pigs. Not a fun situation for the pig or the family it was supposed to

Meshach Browning and a friend demonstrate extreme turkey hunting. *From* Forty-four Years in the Life of a Hunter.

feed for the winter. And panthers and wolves were considered "devils" that would eat livestock, dogs and the occasional settler. Not to mention the fact that Meshach earned up to a healthy thirty dollars a scalp for wolves as per a bounty set by the local courts.

The always industrious and energetic Meshach also took to hauling venison and animal skins into Baltimore, where he cut quite a figure with his buckskin-clothed, rough-hewn appearance, and Annapolis, where he famously gagged on oysters. And Meshach was nothing if not thrifty. He recounts fishing a piece of shot out of a panther's brain, reforming it into a ball and using it to shoot a deer before fishing it out again to repeat the process.

But don't get the idea that Meshach was the epitome of frontiersman infallibility. Common sense was not his strong suit. He exhibited a strange tendency to get lost—often not all that far from his own house—once set himself on fire by firing a flintlock at a bear inside a cave and even managed to get himself stuck to a tree by his hair for a considerable length of time. Nor should you get the idea that Meshach was an unfeeling Neanderthal; in his memoir, he unselfconsciously described himself as crying on several occasions, and he was very devoted to his wife, Mary, (and his second wife, also conveniently named Mary). He wrote lovely, heartfelt poems upon their deaths.

Speaking of the first Mary, she was a frontierswoman if there ever was one. In addition to bearing Meshach eleven kids, she lived with her husband in a variety of *Better Hovel and Cabins* five-star abodes over the years, including one that, as described by her husband, "consisted of the remains of an old cabin, which had been torn down to the joists by hunters and burnt for firewood" and in which "the first thing which greeted us was a very large rattlesnake," as well as one that was "a small house ten feet by twelve in size." But before you feel too sorry for Mary, who was described by her poetic husband as "having clear blue eyes, expressive of the wildness of a fawn in its most playful moments," you should know that she was more than up to the challenge. Once, having sent a horse loaded with the bloody meat of a freshly killed bear home ahead of him, Meshach arrived at their cabin to discover that Mary had led the horse into the house and cut the ropes securing the meat so that it fell right on the floor. Before you question the fair Mary's housekeeping skills, bear in mind that "first she laid skins on the floor, to keep the grease off the boards." On another occasion, the playful bride amused herself by feeding her picky eater of a husband opossum and telling him it was duck. Her final tough-as-hand-forged-nails act was to suggest a replacement wife for Meshach from her deathbed.

While the woman that Mary suggested to him didn't pan out, another Mary soon appeared, and Meshach married again. He lived to the age of seventy-eight and, what with the eleven children, left behind many descendants, including a son, John, who also earned quite a reputation as a sportsman. John Lynn Browning, it was said, was maimed by the cut of a butcher knife in a struggle with a bear (which implies either the bear had a knife or John Lynn was extremely clumsy), but he continued to display great hunting prowess even with his disability. The Brownings were also famous for their violin skills.

If you have a strong stomach, you should read *Forty-four Years of the Life of a Hunter* to get real insight into what it took to not only survive but also enjoy life in the wilds of early Western Maryland, which, for the Brownings, included grit, a sense of humor, a sharp knife and a really good recipe for opossum.

# THE WIZARD OF SOUTH MOUNTAIN

If Michael Zittle Jr. were around today, he'd probably be starring in his own reality TV show (cue the theme song, most likely Heart's "Magic Man" but maybe the Rolling Stones "Sympathy for the Devil"). Melodramatically referred to as "the high priest of all this evil" by South Mountain maven

Madeleine Dahlgren, Zittle was credited by others as having the power to cure sickness. The method Zittle used to bring about these cures is also the reason he came to be known as "Wizard Zittle." It seems M.Z., as Western Marylanders like to call him, was into some magical, spell-casting stuff. Throw into the mix a complex storyline full of colorful and combative relatives, and you've got yourself a hit.

It all started, like so many South Mountain stories, in the old country: Pennsylvania. Okay, really Germany, but with a stopover in Pennsylvania. Zittle's parents, Michael Sr. and Magdalena, migrated from Pennsylvania's Dutchland to Maryland during the 1700s and settled in what would blossom into Zittlestown, a modest little hamlet of rustic homes clustered along South Mountain just outside Boonsboro along the National Road. And the Zittles brought with them a slew of traditions and beliefs steeped in Pennsylvania Dutch superstitions.

Michael Zittle Jr. can blame his bad reputation on Madeleine Dahlgren, who lived and wrote just a stone's throw away from Zittlestown during the late 1800s, but we also have to give her credit for the fact that Zittle is remembered at all. And considering that she called him "evil," Dahlgren actually seemed quite enthralled by Zittle; as a matter of fact, she saved the "Wizard of South Mountain" for the grand finale of her book, *South Mountain Magic*.

Today, intriguing questions remain about Michael Zittle Jr. Did he really dabble in the black arts? Did he commit sacrilege, as Dahlgren maintained? And what was in that notorious "black book" of his, anyway?

Michael Zittle Jr., sometimes also referred as "the Wizard of Zittlestown," was what we think of today as a folk healer, and with things being what they were in rural areas in the early 1800s, it's no wonder people turned to men like Zittle. In Western Maryland in 1830, there was no hopping into the car and driving to the Urgent Care, and certainly no googling things like "sore oozing yellow puss = death?" During a time when a simple cut could lead to infection and morbidity; farming, mining and hunting accidents were everyday occurrences; and diseases easily cured today were fraught with doom, naturally injury and illness brought feelings of desperation.

And as it turns out, the denizens of South Mountain may have had more than an average need for medical intervention. According to research related by Paula M. Strain in *The Blue Hills of Maryland*, many of the settlers of Zittlestown and their descendants have suffered from a rare disorder known on the mountain as Harshman's disease. Today, this disease is identified as familial amyloidosis, a disorder that can affect major organs and causes pain, numbness and weakness. Scary stuff even today, just imagine what it was like for folks suffering from it during Zittle's time. According to Strain's 1993 book, at least 150 descendants of one of the founding families of Zittlestown have suffered from amyloidosis. So those folks leading their hardscrabble lives there on the mountain must have thanked their lucky stars not only that they had their own wizard but also that he had a secret weapon: the magical spell book.

Wielding this mysterious book (and by the way, the Pennsylvania Dutch didn't call them spells, they called them "pow-wows"), Zittle was said to have cured not only friends and neighbors but also folks who had traveled from far and wide seeking his help. Today, we know that this so-called conjuring book, titled *The Friend in Need; Or, Secret Science*, had been anonymously printed in Germany but was said to be a translation of an even older Spanish book. Presumably, the book had come from Europe with the Zittles, but no one really knows for certain. But we do know that M.Z. did a very interesting thing with this spell book. In 1845, he had his own revised version printed

Meet the Zittles. This undated photo of unidentified Zittles is labeled "Home Place"; a note on the back says, "One of the first homes built in Zittlestown." Notice the scissor hanging next to the door—this is a "pow-wow," believed to protect the home from evil. *Courtesy of the Douglas Bast Collection.*

in English. Although he supposedly had "hundreds of copies" printed in Boonsboro, only one of these has survived. And oddly, Dahlgren, living on the edge of Zittlestown only forty years later (M.Z. died about a year after Dahlgren moved to the area), was apparently unable to come across even a single copy. As for the original German book, the one Zittle carried and worked from, it is believed to have been the only copy that ever made it to the United States. (Another version of the original German book was published by John George Hohman in Pennsylvania in the early 1800s.)

In the 1800s, the hills of South Mountain were alive with the sound of Zittles. Like any good country family, they liked to stay together, hence Zittlestown. As the Zittles started adding up, it became apparent they were to be a colorful bunch. For instance, it wasn't enough that there was one wizard in the family; M.Z.'s neighboring niece married a man known as "Professor Mitchell." Mitchell wasn't a real professor, but he did like titles, and after marrying into the Zittles, he found a new but not very original one for himself: "Wizard of South Mountain." Yes, folks, there were not one but two wizards on South Mountain. But these two conjurers practiced very different types of magic. Wizard Mitchell was more of what we today might call a kiddie-party magician—that is, if you consider raising the dead to be appropriate entertainment at children's birthday parties. Mitchell advertised his performances in ads that used phrases like "necromancy, etc.," which really makes you wonder what the "etc." part could have been.

Another interesting character in the Zittle family tree was a nephew of M.Z.'s named Ed Zittle. Now, we do know that the South Mountain area was notoriously haunted, but we're not sure even that accounts for the tale that Ed related to the local newspaper. As reported in the appropriately named *Boonsboro Oddfellow*:

> *Ed Zittle says he saw a spook near the mountain recently. It was like a man, but minus a head, and brandished a flowing tail four miles long with a coffee pot canon on the end. He fired his revolver at it, and Mr. Spook has never been heard of since.*

Sadly, there were no details as to what exactly a "coffee pot canon" was, but apparently, Ed was a frequent visitor to the offices of the newspaper, for in 1875, under the heading "Unpleasantness," they wrote:

> *Dr. Ed Zittle,* [Ed was obviously the most ambitious of the Zittles, bestowing on himself the fake title of "Dr."] *the inventor*

*of the celebrated "coffee-pot canon," stepped into our office on Monday. A single glance at the Beau Hickman* [Beau Hickman was a well-known figure of the day, a would-be dandy famous for freeloading, blackmailing and generally being a lot like most of the people on today's reality shows] *of classic Zittlestown told us that he had been hanging on the ragged edge of some sad calamity. Over his eye was cut a tea biscuit; his nose resembled a bologna sausage, with a congaroo dip in the centre; his neck was encased in flannel rags, and his voice sounded like the croaking of a frog—distress was pictured on every feature of the unfortunate youth.*

*"What in the world is the matter?" we asked.*

*"Ah, Captain," said he with a sigh. "I've seen times; I've been treated badly!" And then he went on to relate how he had a difficulty with Professor Mitchell, the South Mountain Wizard, on last Sunday, and had been knocked down and kicked in the face and head until he was almost dead. All this occurred at Aunt Lid Zittle's house in Zittlestown, while Ed was there on a visit to see his uncle. He says he got away as fast as he could, but not until he had been badly punished, as before stated. We believe suit was brought against Mitchell for assault and battery, but did not hear of his arrest.*

The article doesn't say what provoked Professor Mitchell to beat up poor Ed, but I'm sure it must have been something quite interesting. If only those "Meet the Zittles" video cameras could have been there to capture it. (A public service announcement about violence and anger management would run along with it, of course.)

When M.Z. died, he bequeathed his famous spell book to his son-in-law Simon Summers. Either the spell book failed him or he wasn't a true believer, for poor Simon Summers died of consumption shortly thereafter at the age of forty. Superstition ran deep among the Zittle clan, though, and it was right after Summers's death that its darker side reared its head on South Mountain. As related by Dahlgren in *South Mountain Magic*, Simon Summers didn't stay buried long:

*After his death, it became necessary to put cotton in his nostrils, ears, and mouth, and in this condition he was duly buried. Some days after the funeral his widow, who was a daughter of Michael Zittle, the so-called "wizard," was informed of the circumstance about the cotton, and she became greatly agitated and alarmed in consequence. She asserted that if the dead man should swallow the least portion of this cotton, the entire family, and even his friends, would of necessity, die. To allay her fears and anguish of mind, and possibly because the apprehensions of the relatives were aroused, the body was resurrected in order to replace the cotton. It was thought by others that, had this precaution been neglected, some convulsion of nature, that might have shaken old South Mountain from summit to base, must have occurred!!*

Coming back to that infamous spell book, there was long a great deal of mystery and speculation surrounding Zittle's magic book, and again, much of that speculation was stirred up by Ms. Dahlgren. Actually, Dahlgren was so obsessed with Zittle and his book that at one point, she managed to pry it away from an old woman, under circumstances that were—well, judge for yourself:

*The way in which we happened to see the original book was quite accidental. We called to see an old woman who was considered a "doctress." She was ill, and we found her much troubled because someone had robbed her. But she said that she was trying the various conjurations of the "black book" with the expectation of discovering the thief and thus being able to regain her stolen property. She mentioned to us that the "wizard" had lent her the book for that purpose. We had often heard this book alluded to as the "conjuring book" and were curious to see it, and we obtained a very reluctant consent from this old woman to take it home for a few days only.*

During the time she had the spell book, Dahlgren feverishly attempted to translate it, and despite declaring that the book was profane and the "conjurations" satanic, she copied as much as she could and published it in her own book. Not long after this, it seems Wizard Zittle's original spell book, as well as all the copies he had supposedly had printed, mysteriously vanished from history for quite a long time.

In the 1950s, a gothic horror writer named George Wetzel happened upon a copy of *South Mountain Magic*. He was so intrigued by Wizard Zittle and his black book that he visited the area, shaking down various Zittle descendants for any information that might lead him to the mysterious spell books. He never did find the books, but he did score some inside info passed down in the Zittle family. Wetzel reported, "My informant, Mr. W.S. Zittle, wrote that he asked his mother years ago about the conjure book, and she replied that Uncle Mike used to cure people of their ills by laying on of hands and saying certain words."

Der

Freund in der Noth,

oder

Geheime

Sympathetische Wissenschaft.

Aus dem Spanischen übersetzt,

Psalm 40 spricht der HErr :

Rufe mich an in der Noth, so will ich dich
erretten und du sollst mich preisen—oder
wie andere sagen im 50sten Psalm.

Gedruckt für die Käufer, 1826.

This mysterious magic spellboook was used by Michael Zittle—also known as "the Wizard of South Mountain"—during the 1800s. Zittle was credited with curing mountain folk of various illnesses, but some feared the wizard's powers. *Courtesy of the Boonsboro Museum of History.*

So what's in a magic and possibly evil spell book? I have seen the contents of the book that Zittle published, the one that's in English (and no, I didn't have to extort any sick old ladies to get it), and it begins just the way you'd least expect a book of black magic to begin, with a quote from the Bible: "The Lord sayeth call upon me in the day of trouble and I will deliver thee and thou shalt glorify me." And as for Zittle's "spells," unfortunately there is not much that would be of use here in the twenty-first century—that is, unless you happen to be having a lot of problems with horse thieves or find yourself frequently getting bitten by rabid dogs, in which case you may want to consider moving to a better neighborhood. Supposedly, there are incantations that are a bit more intriguing, such as "How to divine the time of one's death," in the German book.

Finally, there is one more thing to keep in mind about Michael Zittle Jr. The Wizard of South Mountain didn't charge for his services. For M.Z., curing folks and helping his fellow citizens with their problems was a calling. In his later years, when he fell on somewhat hard times (the wizard pension plan hadn't quite gotten off the ground, apparently), Zittle did resort to accepting some fees for his services, but he later believed doing so had brought him bad luck.

Today, if you are curious about Wizard Zittle, you can visit the Boonsboro Museum of History because, happily, both of Wizard Zittle's lost spell books reside there. The small volumes emerged from local attics a few decades ago, and at the Boonsboro Museum, you can check them out in person; they are displayed safe and sound behind glass, along with other wonderful and curious artifacts associated with South Mountain magic.

# HENRY KYD DOUGLAS

## *The Rebel Dandy Who Lost It in Maryland*

Rain poured down, muddying the roads of Washington County. A handsome, well-dressed youth making his way home in the downpour encountered an older gentleman, a neighbor he knew by the name of Isaac Smith. The man was having trouble maneuvering his overloaded two-horse wagon along the messy roads, and the younger man, being somewhat of a Southern gentleman by upbringing, was only too happy to help. He dashed to his own nearby home, quickly returning with horses and a servant. Soon, Smith and his very heavy

When Henry Kyd Douglas left his family plantation in Maryland to enlist in the Confederate army, he began a colorful military career that included serving on Stonewall Jackson's staff and becoming embroiled in many controversial incidents—at least one of which continues to confound historians. *Courtesy of the Douglas Bast Collection.*

wagon were back on their way. The young man recalled, "I was much impressed with the grateful simplicity of the venerable actor as we parted in the rain and mud, with many dignified thanks on his part."

But all was not as it seemed. What the young man—who was named Henry Kyd Douglas and who would soon rise to fame as the youngest member of Stonewall Jackson's staff—didn't know was that "Isaac Smith" was the alias of one John Brown. And on that rainy day in 1859, Douglas's strange, bedraggled neighbor had been transporting not miner's tools in his overloaded wagon, as he had told the youth, but some of the 950 pikes he'd had made to equip the army of slaves he was sure would join him in his planned insurrection at Harpers Ferry.

By the time all was said and done, Douglas himself would gain notoriety for what some consider a tendency to exaggerate his own importance, for his somewhat flamboyant proclivities and, most intriguingly, for possibly having inadvertently contributed to another event of national import—the defeat of the South during the Maryland Campaign of 1862. The dashing young officer and his Forrest Gump–like exploits are, to this day, the subject of great debate among Civil War historians. His poor judgment and pretentiousness, though, are legendary.

Henry Kyd Douglas's connection with John Brown didn't end when he accidently assisted with Brown's preinsurrection weapon smuggling; the twenty-one-year-old managed to be present when J.E.B. Stuart brought the defeated Brown out of the engine house in Harpers Ferry. Characteristically, Douglas was unimpressed by the dramatic firefight and the capture of Brown; he commented, "I did not take much notice of Brown after he came out of his 'Fort,' for I was more interested in Colonel Lewis Washington." Washington was one of Brown's hostages and apparently something of a dandy—a quality to which Douglas aspired: "I recall my admiration of his suavity when, walking quietly away from the fort with some excited friends, he took from his pocket a pair of dark-green kid gloves and began pulling them on." According to Douglas, "merriment abounded" as Washington coolly accepted a friend's invitation to hit the local tavern. Douglas, one imagines, went off in search of a pair of green kid gloves for himself.

John Brown, under the alias Isaac Smith, lived in Washington County while he was preparing for his raid on Harpers Ferry. It was there that Henry Kyd Douglas, future aide to Confederate general Stonewall Jackson, encountered Brown. *Author's collection.*

The young Douglas had just begun work at a law firm in St. Louis when the Civil War broke out. He returned home to Ferry Hill, a mansion poised in a precarious spot on the bluffs between Maryland and what was then Shepherdstown, Virginia, only to find his Southern-sympathizing mother sewing uniform shirts suspiciously in his size, all too ready to send her sacrificial lamb off to war. Thus began the military career that would result in the memoir *I Rode with Stonewall*, or as some folks say it should be called, *Stonewall Rode with Me*.

From his memoirs, readers could get the idea that while Douglas seemed to be everywhere during the war, he was often more impressed by who wore what than by military events. According to him, battles were either exceedingly dull (he called the Battle of Malvern Hill, a Southern loss, "painfully monotonous") or, in the case of battles he participated in and that the South won, fantastically exciting. But his war stories often featured reminisces involving clothing. In Maryland shortly before the Battle of Antietam, Douglas had a new hat with a "beautiful plume" shot off his head, and he went back a little while later, risking more Yankee bullets, to retrieve it. He was sidelined by a fever at Fredericksburg, but on seeing Stonewall Jackson from his sickbed, he made note of the general's new uniform. Other than that, he didn't have much to say about that battle, except that "there was nothing interesting about the Battle of Fredericksburg." At Chancellorsville he claimed that he had sat with the wounded Jackson and gave the soon-to-die general the play by play of the fighting. But however preoccupied he may have been with appearances, he was no shirker; he was severely wounded at Gettysburg and wounded numerous other times during the war.

Douglas ended the war with his usual aplomb. His troops fired the last shot at Appomattox and were also the last to stack their arms after the Confederate surrender. But Douglas's clashes with the Yankees didn't end with the war.

Immediately following his parole in 1865, Douglas couldn't resist temptation when a Shepherdstown girl asked him to don his Confederate uniform—strictly prohibited for a parolee—and pose for a portrait at a photographer's studio. Thanks to a local tattletale (or maybe just the concern of someone who was made uneasy by Douglas's parading around in Rebel garb after pledging his loyalty to the Union), the recently retired officer was promptly arrested for violation of parole. For Douglas, however, having a police escort show up at his door was a welcome bit of attention. "This had the taste of pleasing excitement, for life was already getting very monotonous," he wrote. He was less amused when he was sentenced to two months at Fort Delaware for the transgression—a punishment he declared "lame." But this trip to prison took an unexpected and serious detour. Douglas suddenly found himself implicated in the assassination of President Lincoln.

There's no need to worry for the welfare of our hero. Sporting a blasé attitude, the arrested Douglas, as usual, made out pretty well and even managed to enjoy the Grand Review of the Army of the Republic parade through Washington, all while savoring a "drawn-out breakfast" at a restaurant with his guard.

To hear Douglas describe it, he was more lodger than prisoner in what he called his "comfortable room" adjoining accused conspirator Mary Surratt's cell at the penitentiary as he waited for the little misunderstanding to be cleared up. It seemed a turncoat Union officer who had once been part of Douglas's brigade (perhaps in an attempt to save face after the war) claimed to have seen John Wilkes Booth in Stonewall Jackson's camp at one point and had implicated Douglas and several other officers. Douglas, meanwhile, was enjoying his proximity to the sensational trial. He said he found Mary Surratt "attractive," describing her as "fair, fat and forty."

After what he cavalierly called "three weeks of exciting and interesting confinement," Douglas was released and wasted no time in offending his detractors by going directly from prison to a shop on Pennsylvania Avenue, where he left sporting a "fine soft hat of Confederate grey." He was soon arrested again for the photograph affair (he was arrested "about once a week," he said), and he finally landed in Fort Delaware, a prison camp that he described as a "summer resort" and where, he claimed, he taught the commandant how to handle his new horses and dined with the officer's family. And then at last, Henry Kyd Douglas, Confederate bon vivant, was finally free to return home to Ferry Hill.

As we've seen, Douglas's Civil War career was certainly as colorful as they come. Before we end our visit with good ol' Henry, there's one little misadventure we have left out. It seems there was a mysterious incident that occurred during that all-important Maryland Campaign of 1862—the campaign that culminated in the Battle of Antietam. The incident was one that would, as they say, live in infamy. The main suspect was none other than our buddy Henry Kyd Douglas. It seems that Douglas may have lost something a great deal more important during the Maryland Campaign than just his hat.

The incident in question was an epic blunder. On September 13, a Union corporal found a document wrapped around three cigars lying in a field outside Frederick. The document was a copy of Special Orders 191—today known as "Lost Order 191"—composed by Robert E. Lee and addressed to General D.H. Hill. It gave detailed locations and movements of the Army of Northern Virginia for its ongoing invasion of Maryland. Union General McClellan, on being presented the document, is said to have exclaimed, "Here is a paper with which, if I cannot whip Bobby Lee, I will be willing to go home!" The outcome of the Maryland Campaign was extremely important in American history—as in resulted in the Emancipation Proclamation important. Special Orders 191 falling into Union hands was arguably one of the important pieces of that outcome.

History left a big question mark as to who the butter-fingered culprit in the affair was, but many historians have long suspected Douglas. As an aide to Jackson, Douglas was not only routinely given the task of delivering documents but was also, in this case, the local boy who knew the area, making him even likelier to have been the courier dispatched over the Maryland hills. And not long after the special orders blunder, Douglas was "re-assigned" and rode with Stonewall no more. In his memoir, Douglas only cagily addressed the issue of Special Orders 191, casually calling it "an accident never yet explained."

It's too bad, one might think, Douglas didn't keep a diary during the war. But actually, he did. Several soldiers did, as a matter of fact. And, most interestingly, they are still around.

Adding to the Douglas controversy are several small, timeworn journals in which the young Confederate scribbled diligently during the war. Today, these diaries are owned by Doug Bast, who owns the Boonsboro Museum of History. According to Bast, the Douglas diary from 1862 is no smoking musket. As you probably won't be surprised to hear, there is no "Dear Diary: today I did something really, really stupid" entry from September 13, 1862.

Even if Henry Kyd Douglas did lose the Lost Order, he was not necessarily the pretentious brat he is often portrayed as being. It seems Douglas's bravado was paired with an unlikely guilelessness; after all, he didn't exactly have anything to gain by admitting he helped John Brown transport those pikes. And unlike almost everyone else who participated in the Civil War, Douglas, though he wrote about his war experiences often for periodicals, never published his memoir. Indeed, it wasn't until his nephew, who inherited Douglas's estate, published them some thirty-seven years after his uncle's death that they saw the light of day.

In his final years, Henry Kyd Douglas, who never married, reigned alone at Ferry Hill. A beloved fiancée, sent overseas by a family who didn't want her marrying the former Rebel, died of "Roman fever" (aka malaria). The sentimental Douglas penned poetry in her honor as well as to a beloved blind horse that perished falling off the cliffs near Ferry Hill.

Douglas ran a successful law firm in downtown Hagerstown, where, it is said, the Civil War veteran who had ridden with Stonewall was sometimes seen walking the streets in all his dandified glory, a yellow rose clenched in his teeth.

# Harris the Crazy Naked Guy

## *Honorable Mention*

He was a middle-aged Quaker of "quiet demeanor" and "humble manners." And he liked to walk through the streets of Cumberland stark naked.

He made his first appearance in the spring of 1828 and created quite a sensation among the folks of Cumberland when he marched into town, stood in the middle of the street and began stripping off his clothes. And perhaps this is the reason he was also described as being "of good physical proportions."

His name was Harris, and he was believed to be from somewhere in the vicinity of Leesburg, Virginia. But each spring, it seemed, the humble Quaker found himself compelled to visit Cumberland to tear off his clothes in public. Harris's hobby of disrobing and "parading the streets in a nude state" was accompanied by a lot of preaching and prophesying about what the naked man called a "terrible calamity" that was soon to come.

Year after year, like the first robin of spring, Harris made his appearance, and each year, the good people of Cumberland were really quite tolerant of their naked visitor. He was put into jail once after marching naked up the aisle of a local church during services, but he was soon turned loose. Eventually, the citizens of Cumberland gave a collective well-what-are-ya-gonna-do sigh. Local historian William Lowdermilk wrote during the 1800s:

> It was finally resolved that he should be permitted to have his walk out, the hope being entertained that he would then regard his mission as fulfilled, and cease to annoy the people.

Lowdermilk continued:

> The visits of this singular man extended over a period of nearly five years, and shortly after their cessation the great fire of 1833 took place, which is said to have consumed all the houses along the route he so persistently paraded.

And the moral of this, folks, is if a crazy naked guy comes parading through your town prophesying a catastrophic event, you might just want to put some fresh batteries into your smoke detector and make a donation to your local fire department because sometimes, the crazy naked guy is right.

# Part 4

# Miscellaneous Mayhem, Mysterious Places and Mythical Mountains

*His body was dissected by the physicians, and "Old Joe Shumate," a curious old character, got a part of the skin and tanned it, and it is said the leather was exceedingly pliable.*
—*J. Thomas Scharf*

We have a lot of stops to make on this part of our trip through mysterious Western Maryland, and some of them aren't for the squeamish. We're going to introduce you to a few severed limbs, hang out at a couple of hangings, visit a fort with a very dark history and step back in time for several other unexpected adventures. Prepare to be surprised, amused and possibly a little grossed out. Buckle your seatbelts, the first stop is coming right up.

## A TALE OF TWO SEVERED ARMS

Now, friends, we are going to duck back into the National Museum of Civil War Medicine in Frederick, as well as the Boonsboro Museum of History, because, it turns out, they have a few more treasures. Treasures in the form of an unmatched pair of severed arms, that is.

In January 2012, the National Museum of Civil War Medicine in Frederick received a very unusual donation: a mummified arm. This

This severed arm made the rounds before finding its forever home at the National Museum of Civil War Medicine in Frederick. It's believed to have belonged to a very young casualty of the Battle of Antietam. *Courtesy of the National Museum of Civil War Medicine.*

wasn't just your average, run-of-the-mill mummified arm. It was one with a long and colorful history, and one that arrived with more questions than answers.

Displayed for years in Sharpsburg at a museum operated by John G. Ray as the "Human Arm Found on the Antietam Battlefield," this arm, pardon the expression, changed hands many times over the years. And what is known of the arm begins, naturally, with a love story.

Dr. John Gaines came to Maryland in the fall of 1862 with the Confederate army. As an assistant surgeon, he had his work more than cut out for him after the Battle of Antietam. Unfortunately, he also soon found himself left behind as a prisoner of war. But Gaines lucked out on two points. He was exchanged after only six weeks, and before he left town, he managed to win the affection of the daughter of Dr. Otho Smith, a Boonsboro physician.

After the war, Dr. Gaines returned to Washington County, went into practice with Dr. Smith and married the doctor's daughter. It is said that the arm first emerged after Smith's death, when his son found it wrapped up in a piece of cloth in his father's attic. Since both Smith and his son-in-law had cared for soldiers after the Battle of Antietam, the son assumed the arm had come from a soldier who had been wounded or killed during the fall of 1862.

After being liberated from the attic, the arm got around, spending time with both Wilmer Mumma and Grafton Smith, both of whose ancestors had owned property on the Antietam Battlefield, before winding up at Ray's museum, where it was a much-loved macabre reminder of war for many years. At Ray's museum, more stories about the arm seemed to accumulate; one maintained that it had been dug up on the battlefield by a farmer's plow, and another told that it was found sitting on a stone wall on the site. Despite these assertions, no one was ever quite sure if it even really was an authentic artifact from the 1862 battle. Finally, Ray's museum closed, and the arm eventually was donated to the National Museum of Civil War Medicine.

Curator Lori Eggleston was naturally intrigued by the museum's newest and possibly most gruesome artifact; not only did she want to try to find out if the arm really belonged to a soldier killed at Antietam, but she also had concerns as to whether the arm was safe to handle and display. Supposedly, the arm had been embalmed; if this was true, it could be harboring some very hazardous chemicals. And so the arm made yet another trip, this time from Frederick to the Museum of Natural History in D.C. for extensive testing

This testing revealed that the arm had not been embalmed and that any mummification had occurred naturally somehow. It was also determined that the arm had most likely come from a very young man, probably a youth around sixteen years old. Unfortunately, the current age of the arm could not be determined, but based on the injuries the arm and hand show, the age and sex of its owner and what is known of the arm's background, the limb is still believed to be an authentic relic of the Battle of Antietam. The arm is expected to be on display at the museum soon and will probably have at last found its final resting place in a nice exhibit there.

Unlike the first arm, the appendage at the Boonsboro Museum of History has been in one place for quite a while. Displayed with a bullet lodged between its gristly ligaments "for dramatic effect," the arm has graced the wall of the museum for decades. It's quite a favorite with visitors, and sometimes the arm's reputation precedes it, as on one occasion when a family arrived with a cherubic blond six-year-old daughter in tow. "I want to see that arm!" the youngster demanded. Her parents explained they had read about the museum and its holdings in a book about "offbeat places" and the severed arm had been all the girl had talked about since. The little girl was not disappointed. There it was, in all its gruesome glory, lit by a flickering fluorescent bulb, showing off its still-intact fingernails and charming remnants of gristle and shards of torn bone—all glistening beneath a weird, maple-colored glaze.

The Boonsboro arm also has a murky background, mostly because before it found a home at the Boonsboro Museum it was in the proud possession of a "secret society" in Washington County. Apparently, the society in question wants to remain secret, and its name is well guarded. What is known is what it was that the secret society did with its severed arm: "initiation ceremonies." Perhaps it is better not to know what exactly those entailed, but we do know that museum owner Doug Bast acquired the rest of the skeleton along with the arm. He believes it was originally a medical skeleton and that it predates the Civil War. The arm is the only part on display in the museum because, oddly, it was the only part of the skeleton that retained pieces of flesh and, thus, has that icky, glazed-ham-from-hell glow.

And so, while there might still be more questions than answers about Western Maryland's two beloved severed arms, the mystery of the arm at the Museum of Civil War Medicine continues to be unraveled. As for our friend the arm in Boonsboro, visitors, including small angelic girls, continue to be enchanted by it. You might want to pack up the family, hit the road, visit both arms and find out for yourself just what's so charming about Western Maryland's severed limbs.

## WASHINGTON MONUMENT WEIRDNESS

Something came over the residents of Boonsboro on July 4, 1827. Call it patriotic fervor. Call it a case of mass ADHD. Call it no one had invented hotdogs and air-conditioned movie theaters yet. Whatever it was, according to the *Hagerstown Torch Light*, it manifested itself like this:

> *The citizens of Boonsboro assembled at the public square on the 4th instant, at half-past seven o'clock in the morning, to ascend the "Blue Rocks," for the patriotic purpose of erecting a monument to the memory of him whose name stands at the head of this article.*

The article was entitled "Washington Monument, Near Boonsboro," and, yes, the citizens of Boonsboro had decided to construct a really large monument out of rocks in honor of George Washington. And build it they did on that fateful July 4—sort of. The article, referenced in *Scharf's History of Western Maryland* in the 1800s, is followed by this comment from the renowned historian: "It does not appear that the Washington monument referred to above was ever completed according to the intention of the zealous projectors, and at the present day the novel structure is in ruins." To read the accounts of the day, however, the monument builders seemed quite satisfied with themselves and, mission accomplished after that single day's fervor, rested most contentedly on their laurels.

Today, of course, the stone tower known as the Washington Monument stands firmly and proudly atop the "blue rocks" of South Mountain, a favorite area landmark, a popular stop for Appalachian Trail hikers and a testament to what a zealous mob with a day off work can accomplish. But quite a bit has transpired on that rocky pinnacle between that hot July morning and today, and much of it is really entertaining.

The folks in Washington County, as evidenced by the county's name, had a thing for a certain founding father, and ol' George returned the favor by stopping by Hagerstown in 1790, a visit he spent doing a whole lot of toasting and holding forth on this and that. Hagerstown planned to construct a statue in honor of Washington in 1821. According to Scharf, "It was proposed to erect a statue to Gen. Washington in the public square, but no further action appears to have been taken in the matter." That plan actually did progress as far as collecting $106 for the statue, which was going to involve a lot of marble and a fountain. But the whole thing stalled out, and the money ultimately went toward the Washington Monument in D.C. So really you have to give the citizens of Boonsboro credit for their full day's worth of patriotic follow-through.

It was not unusual for Washington County residents to celebrate the Fourth of July in a big way. As Scharf related of Hagerstown's Fourth of July in 1810:

> *It was observed with a parade, volleys of artillery, and a dinner at the Cold Spring south of town. The cannon used was a large one, which lay unmounted on the hill just east of the town. It subsequently burst, killing one man, George Bower, and so seriously wounding another, George Gelwig, that his leg had to be amputated.*

All this was quite memorable, but it wasn't until that crowd gathered in Boonsboro on July 4, 1827, that Washington County really displayed the extent of its devotion to its namesake. No one knows for certain where the idea originated. Perhaps it was in the town hall or, more likely, the town tavern. And it appears there was at least a smidge of forethought because some sort of foundation was laid for the monument ahead of time.

In what may be the Western Maryland understatement of the 1800s, the *Torch Light* reported that, as the would-be monument builders made their way to the appointed spot in Boonsboro on the morning of July 4, 1827, "The men seemed actuated by a spirit of zeal and ardor almost bordering on enthusiasm."

And if there was ever a convenient locale for a spontaneously erected monument, this was it. Perched on the side of South Mountain amid a jumble of large rocks, the spot chosen for the monument overlooked a wide expanse of the beautiful Cumberland Valley. Those pragmatic Boonsboro fellows were no fools. They figured they'd use the rocks that were already lying around to construct their monument, which sure beat hauling tons and tons of heavy stone up the mountain. And so off they marched, an impromptu parade complete with flag, fife and drums—full of patriotism and ready for a hard day's labor.

Local accounts go to great lengths to point out that no one was intoxicated during this endeavor; they point it out so much, in fact, that one assumes it was frequently suggested they must have been pretty loaded to do what they did that day. These men, sober as they were said to be, labored throughout the morning, and they were apparently quite put out by some men from nearby Frederick, who showed up and "stood aloof from the work" but "ate and drank" and generally displayed a much more modern understanding of how to observe a holiday.

The monument builders broke for lunch and were subjected to a speech by a Mr. Clinghan, described as "a gentleman of the revolutionary period" who was "rendered infirm by age and ill-health." Thus reinspired, the men resumed their rock stacking until four o'clock, at which point there was a reading of the Declaration of Independence, and that was pretty much it. The guys returned home, and those who had been involved proceeded to do a whole lot of talking about the day's events, the hard work involved and, again, how "not one of them returned home intoxicated."

If you are wondering what the results of approximately eight hours of back-breaking work by a very inspired group of patriotic guys looks like, this quote from a 1906 history of Washington County probably sums it up: "No observant stranger…fails to inquire what it is, and but few citizens can give any satisfactory reply."

The monument-builders, on the other hand, described it this way:

*This monument is fifty-four feet in circumference at its base and fifteen feet high (we contemplate raising it to thirty feet after the busy season is passed). The wall is composed of huge stones, many weighing upwards of a ton, with the whole of the center filled up with the same material.*

*A flight of steps, commencing at the base and running through the body of the fabric, enables us to ascend to the top.*

They then go on to describe the view from atop the monument at great length. The author of this description was nothing if not honest, for he added, "As it was raised in much haste all cannot boast the regular accuracy of perfect beauty." He also went on to say the structure was "rude and naked of all the charms of architecture." Sounds good so far.

One thing missing entirely from the description of the monument erected that day was mention of the mortar holding the structure together, probably because they didn't use any. No, our monument builders simply stacked the rocks on top of each other and hoped for the best. That fall though, as promised, several citizens did follow through and added

Three gentlemen pose at the Washington Monument in one of its periods of dilapidation in this undated photo. *Courtesy of the Douglas Bast Collection.*

The Washington Monument was at its worst in this undated photo. *Courtesy of the Douglas Bast Collection.*

fifteen feet to the monument, but that was the end of the building of the original Washington Monument. And as for the maintenance of the tower, there was none, unless you call people visiting the monument and pushing rocks off it just to hear them crashing down the mountainside maintenance. By the time Colonel E.P. Alexander came across the tower during the Maryland Campaign of 1862, he figured the crumbling structure had once been a windmill.

In 1881, the local Odd Fellows, with some financial assistance from Madeleine Dahlgren, mistress of South Mountain House, "restored" the tower, although "rebuilt" may be a better word. The new tower was replete with an observation deck covered by an awning, was sturdier and had more of a finished appearance than the original. But this new and improved tower was not destined to stand, either. It had already been damaged by lightning strikes (that awning was supported by a steel frame) and was sporting a nice big crack by the early part of the 1900s. Then, insult was added to injury when someone blew the tower up with a stick of dynamite. One story goes that the culprit was a German sympathizer

Although it had a precarious existence for generations, today the Washington Monument is ready for the long haul. *Author's photo.*

who thought blowing up an already ramshackle tower on South Mountain was more constructive than enlisting in the German army. An even more colorful story says that the fetching daughters of a local farmer had gotten into the naughty habit of using the tower for trysts with their lovers. The angry farmer decided to put an end to the romantic shenanigans (and the possibility of undesired grandchildren) by blowing up the tower with a well-placed stick of dynamite. Another version may or may not implicate one Wile E. Coyote. But however it happened, the Washington Monument was once again in ruins.

Enter the Civilian Conservation Corp in 1936. This time the tower was rebuilt to last. The Washington Monument State Park was dedicated on the 109th anniversary of the day that pack of zealous Boonsboro patriots had made their nonintoxicated climb up South Mountain and then made their nonintoxicated way back down several hours later in the shadow of a well-intentioned but haphazard tower.

If you climb the dark, winding stairway to the top of the Washington Monument today, you will most likely be greeted at the top by one of the many binocular-wielding birdwatchers who make regular use of the tower and rewarded with one of the loveliest views imaginable of the Cumberland Valley.

## Macabre Murders and Entertaining Executions

Let's face it, for early Western Marylanders, options for titillating entertainment were limited. Unlike us modern "civilized" folk, they were deprived of the opportunity to enjoy graphic footage of plastic surgery and people smashing folding chairs over one another's heads with the flick of a remote. Hard to imagine, right? So perhaps it's no wonder they turned out in droves for a good old-fashioned execution. I'm still not quite convinced, though, that this completely explains some of the extreme execution antics in early Western Maryland, such as people grappling for a hunk of the hangman's noose. As far as people trying to secure a piece of the executed man's body, I'm equally at a loss to explain their motivations, but I'll suggest that the lack of commemorative execution snow globes and sun visors added to the appeal of these grisly souvenirs. As for the murders that led to the gallows, these were actually not so different from modern murders. A misguided soul committed

The Hagerstown jail is the setting of this 1916 photo. It is believed to have been taken during the execution of a man named John Brown who was convicted of "murdering a widow." This execution was the swan song for the gallows; it was the last time it was used. *Courtesy of the Douglas Bast Collection.*

the occasional murder or murders—sometimes involving decapitation, sometimes not—and everyone else salivated over the gruesome play by play in the daily newspapers.

Not all crimes were violent ones in early Maryland, but for some minor offenses, the punishment could be almost as severe. Take, for instance, the three fellows convicted of stealing a jug of beer during General Braddock's 1755 stay at Fort Cumberland. One of the thirsty soldiers was sentenced to nine hundred lashes while the other two got off easier with a lenient eight hundred lashes each.

When someone got sentenced to death in early Western Maryland, it was usually the result of something along the lines of murdering someone and then making a really inadequate and messy attempt to hide the body.

In the 1800s, people often committed murders for some of the same reasons they do today: sex and money. A case in point on the fornication front is the sensational 1843 murder committed by William S. Chrise. It started when Allegany County resident Chrise got rather put out with one Abraham Frey for being "unduly familiar" with Mrs. Chrise. One thing led to another, and the next thing you know, Frey was discovered with his skull crushed in by a very forceful blow with the business end of a hoe. Chrise was hanged a few months later.

The 1829 murder trial of Washington County sheriff George Swearingen was certainly one of the most titillating of the century. Having undertaken a very passionate relationship with a "lewd woman" named Rachel Cunningham, Swearingen unsuccessfully tried to off his wife by "accidentally" upsetting the buggy she was riding in. When this didn't quite do the trick, the persistent sheriff set up a fake fall from a supposedly unruly horse. This worked better. The sheriff was found dramatically cradling his dead wife at the feet of an indignant horse. The trial that followed involved everything from an examination of the horse's knees to a thorough dissection of the deceased, despite her "advanced state of decomposition." The horse apparently had the better lawyer, and Sheriff Swearingen was sentenced to death.

Robbery was the motive in an 1855 mini murder spree by Frederick Miller in Cumberland. The out-of-towner made the acquaintance of a local physician, Dr. Hadel, and the two men went for a walk, which resulted in Dr. Hadel's head and body becoming separated and sequestered in different locations in the woods. Despite the exertion this must have taken, Miller returned to Dr. Hadel's office with robbery on his mind. That's where he encountered the doctor's friend Henry Groff. Miller quickly talked Groff into also taking a walk down the exact same path, with the same unfortunate outcome. Miller was quickly found out, and within weeks of the murders, he took another walk—this one to the gallows.

In Western Maryland, there was no such thing as a bad day for a hanging. For the 1856 execution of Frederick Miller, even a snowstorm couldn't keep the hordes away:

> *The execution took place near the almshouse, and although the day was bitterly cold, thousands upon thousands of persons flocked through the deep snow to witness the horrible sight.*

For the 1851 dispatch of a wife-murderer named Thomas McLaughlin, "The weather was cool and a slight snow fell. There was a great crowd of people at the scene of the execution, embracing men, women and children, many of whom came from adjoining States." Yes, folks, pack a picnic lunch and throw the kids in the buggy, we're going out of state, in the snow, to watch 'em string someday up.

One can only imagine the traffic snarls around Cumberland for the three-for-one execution of William Cotterill and his two sons, all convicted of relieving an Englishman of a large sum of money and leaving his mangled body in a creek. It may have been the largest turnout in Allegany County execution entertainment history:

> *Friday, February 25th, the day appointed for the execution, was wet and cheerless yet thousands were gathered in the streets of the town and along the roads leading into it…Various estimates have been made of the number present at the execution, ranging from ten thousand to forty thousand.*

It wasn't just the execution itself that lured the stadium-sized crowds. Often, the crowd was treated to a parade, in which the convicted man served as unenthusiastic grand marshal. Then, upon reaching the scaffold, there was singing. And sometimes, even the sentenced got into the festive spirit, such as the affable William Chrise:

> *He walked from the jail to the scaffold, which had been erected on the commons…On the route to the scaffold he was guarded by the "Cumberland Guards" commanded by Captain Alexander King, with a drum and fife in advance. The services at the place of execution were quite lengthy and impressive, several hymns being sung, in all of which*

*the prisoner joined. During the intervals Chrise sat calmly chewing tobacco, occasionally rising from his seat to spit beyond the fatal trap, as though fearing to soil it. Just before the last moment he sang in a clear, loud and unbroken voice, a hymn of which the following couplet is a part:*

*"This is the way I long have sought*
*And mourned because I found it not."*

*The sheriff, Normand Bruce, was deeply affected by the unpleasant duty… and it was doubtless the most painful act of his life. When the rope was cut, several witnesses of the scene fainted, and much excitement prevailed.*

For some, it was after the hanging that the real fun began. After the execution of our friend Chrise, things took a turn for the really, really creepy:

*When life became extinct the body was taken down, and conveyed to the old Court House, where the physicians made some experiments with it. It was afterwards dissected, and Old Joe Shumate, an eccentric man, and one regarded as very wicked, secured a portion of the skin and tanned it, the leather proving very soft and pliable.*

The sinister Mr. Shumate was not the only person to have a good use for the bodies of executed criminals. Dr. Frederick Dorsey was the most respected physician of his day in Western Maryland despite the fact that he was "not a regular graduate of any medical college, although he attended one or two courses of lectures." Perhaps because of his lack of formal training, however, he would sometimes resort to interesting means to secure a dissection subject. After the execution of the Cotterills, the good doctor gleefully absconded with one of the bodies. In the words of a historian who was a contemporary of Dorsey's:

*He came possessed of one of their bodies for dissection—how he rode from point to point to avoid pursuit, with the dead body beside him on the horse, the grim corpse at one moment sitting up erect behind him, and then again dangling down before him like a bag of meal! How it tumbled off and how he struggled to get it back again!*

When they weren't jostling one another for a body to use for wallet making or experimentation, spectators would sometimes try to snag other souvenirs of their fun day:

> *Some of the spectators, we are told, struggled fiercely for fragments of the ropes with which the men were hanged. Their object in striving to get possession of them was to wear them as "charms" against disease or misfortune.*

The hangings continued right up until 1916 in Washington County, when a man named John Brown (no relation) was executed for the murder of a Hagerstown widow. With this swan song, the trusty gallows called it a day, and the citizens of Western Maryland began to turn to more civilized forms of entertainment and more traditional methods of medical training, as well as, presumably, making leather crafts from less exotic sources.

## FORT FREDERICK: FUN AND FEAR ON THE FRONTIER

In the 1750s, an alarming letter appeared in the *Maryland Gazette* from a citizen on "the frontier," i.e., Western Maryland. The letter implored Maryland governor Horatio Sharp to send help, and send it fast:

> *We are in the greatest distress here…Last Friday the Indians killed three men in the gap in the mountains and we have certain accounts that there is a large body of Indians who expect to fall upon this settlement.*

The Indians in question had been desperately fighting to stop the British colonials from encroaching on their lands and, egged on and assisted by the French, their methods had taken a turn for the no-holds-barred. The treatment of the Indians by the settlers was just as brutal. Historian T.C. Williams summed up the hate-hate relationship:

> *The Indians kept up a warfare upon the settlements, scalping and burning and carrying into captivity and being in their turn hunted like wild beasts.*

Governor Sharp was commendably hands-on. He left Annapolis and headed to the wilds of Western Maryland, risking Indian attacks to oversee the building of protective blockhouses throughout Frederick County. But it was soon apparent that stronger fortifications were needed, and Sharp secured six thousand pounds for the building of a stone fort at Big Pool outside Hancock. In 1756, with great urgency, Fort Frederick, encompassing an acre and a half of ground and with walls up to four feet thick in places, was built.

Imagine for a moment being so terrified of what might come out of the woods that you needed to be inside a fort with walls four feet thick, and you'll have some idea of what life was like in Western Maryland in the 1700s. A man called "the trusty Captain Dagworthy" was put in charge of the new fort, and he, in turn, commissioned three hundred soldiers. In case I still haven't given you a sufficient idea of the horror and violence of the times, here's a description of what this small army did with its time:

> *One third were kept on scouting duty to guard the settlements against stealthy attacks from small parties of the enemy, and to fire their zeal a bounty of thirty pounds was offered for every Indian scalp or prisoner brought in by the rangers.*

In 1757 and 1758, refugees from Indian raids arrived and joined the frontiersmen at the fort, where they were all promptly treated to a smallpox

In 1758, local frontiersmen trained troops at Fort Frederick. As experienced Indian fighters, they taught the militiamen how to shoot from the cover of rocks and trees and persuaded them to replace their conspicuously bright red uniforms with frontiersmen-style garb. *Author's collection.*

epidemic. By 1763, it seemed tensions were calming; the fort was even optimistically leased to a local farmer. But the settlers' collective sigh of relief came a bit early. Ironically, it was the end of the French and Indian War that pressed Fort Frederick back into use: Ottawa chief Pontiac, believing the withdrawal of the French would spark the colonists' penetration farther into Indian lands, started his own war of sorts. He united numerous tribes and commenced an all-out assault on the settlers. Over one hundred settlers were killed and thousands more were driven from their homes. Seven hundred of these desperate souls took refuge at Fort Frederick.

Perhaps it was this period that gave birth to one of the fort's most enduring legends, "the Angel of Fort Frederick." The story is a small bright spot in the otherwise dark history of the fort, and it began in London when a young woman named Cecelia Markham, recently orphaned, decided to leave England and follow her betrothed, who was already in America. Unfortunately, things being what they were back then, she didn't know exactly where he was in America but believed he couldn't be that hard to find. The impetuous girl arrived in Annapolis, where she learned that her fiancé was probably "somewhere around" Fort Frederick. She set off hopefully for Western Maryland.

Perhaps she was given bad directions, or maybe finding a particular location in a country she had never been to before, in the wilds of a new frontier no less, wasn't the girl from London's strong suit for some reason. In any event, after much hardship, she finally found herself within sight of Fort Frederick, but on the wrong side of the river. Miss Markham, by this point was, as we say today, pretty much done. Rather than try to find an alternative way to the fort and hopefully her lover, she dove into the river. When watchmen at the fort spied the dark haired figure swimming across, they mistook her for an Indian and waited on the other side with muskets raised. We can only imagine their astonishment when the English maiden emerged (possibly in slow motion), dripping, from the river.

It may have been a good day for the men of Fort Frederick, but unfortunately for Cecelia, her fiancé was nowhere to be found. The always energetic Miss Markham stayed on at the fort, however, and set to work trying to improve conditions at the gloomy place, offering music and sewing lessons and generally charming the put-upon residents into temporarily forgetting their problems.

Finally, the fiancé was located and was "brought to the fort," presumably willingly, although history does not say. The couple was hastily married at Fort Frederick, and having had enough of America with its inconvenient

This July 29, 1902 photo shows a group of merry-makers at the ruins of Fort Frederick. *Courtesy of the Douglas Bast Collection.*

rivers and disgruntled natives, they eventually returned to England, where they may or may not have died from the plague.

Fort Frederick was used as a prison camp during the Revolutionary War and saw a bit of action during the Civil War. After that, the fort was left unattended and stood silent watch over quiet farm fields and peaceful woods. Even as its walls crumbled, it was a popular destination for sightseers and was considered a nice spot for a picnic.

Fort Frederick today serves as a spot for historical reenactments and interpretation—a locale for fun events such as an annual ghost walk and a market fair—and as a striking reminder of what life was like for early Western Marylanders. *Author's photo.*

Merrymakers attend a market fair inside modern Fort Frederick. *Author's photo.*

In 1920, the State of Maryland purchased Fort Frederick, and in the 1930s, the Civilian Conservation Corp went to work restoring it. Today at the Fort Frederick State Park Visitor Center, you can check out the colorful looks once sported by settlers, colonial armies and Indians; they are modeled by some eerie-looking mannequins. You can also visit the fort and the restored barracks, but be warned: there are supposedly ghosts floating around the fort, including a mysterious "Lady in White" and unhappy spirits left over from the smallpox epidemics.

There's always plenty going on at Fort Frederick to keep visitors and any lingering past residents entertained; for example, each spring there is a "market fair" where folks can mingle with fully costumed Indians, frontiersmen, soldiers and even, if they're lucky, a rat catcher with a live rat in tow. And each fall, the fort hosts a fantastically over-the-top "ghost walk," featuring hangings, dismemberments, disembowelments and a monster or two. I have to say that I highly recommend both of these events, as well as visiting the fort on a quiet day when you can experience for yourself being inside the great stone walls and imagine what it must have been like in the days of the early settlers, when four feet of stone could mean the difference between life and death.

## THE SAD DISAPPEARANCE OF COLONEL FRENCH'S PIE

The Confederates seemed to be losing a lot of important (to them) things in Boonsboro during the Maryland Campaign. Henry Kyd Douglas lost a hat that he was so attached to he braved Yankee bullets to go back to retrieve it. And poor Confederate colonel Basset French experienced his own tragic loss while in town in 1862.

The U.S. Hotel, sitting conveniently at the intersection of Boonsboro's main thoroughfare, was a popular stopover for troops of both sides during the Civil War. It seems the landlady, though, must have had a bit of a Southern leaning because not only did she happily entertain Colonel French, a well-known aide to General Robert E. Lee and General Stonewall Jackson, but she also helped to hide French from Union troops. It all started when the colonel, taking a break from all that Rebel army business and whatnot, was happily ensconced at a table in the dining room of the U.S. Hotel, relishing what he called an "excellent" dinner in the company of a young soldier from Louisiana, when his feast was rudely interrupted. He related the dismaying moment in his memoir:

> *I had finished the substantials and with an air of unmistakable satisfaction only to be appreciated by one with a stomach "with fat capon lined" had stretched out my hand for an apple pie when I heard the clatter of cavalry passing the tavern…Dropping the pie I rushed to the window overlooking the Sharpsburg Road and—horrible vision—I saw a troop of Yankee*

> *Cavalry dashing into the National Road, yelling like very devils. Here was a nice "kettle of fish."*

At this point the terrified landlady dashed into the room and "implored [him] for the love of God to seek shelter in her chamber."

This caused the not-so-gallant French to remark:

> *I thought however inviting that might be under other auspices, better chances of escape might be found in other, though less comfortable, place of concealment.*

In short order, an indignant Colonel French found himself secured in a dark basement, where he stayed until the fun-spoiling Federals were chased out by Confederate cavalry, at which point French emerged and high-tailed it back upstairs with high hopes, only to discover that "[his] pie, like the young Louisianan, had vanished."

French survived the Civil War, but the disappointment of the pie that got away at the U.S. Hotel in Boonsboro was significant enough that the traumatized colonel recalled it in his wartime memoir.

Today, you'll find the Vesta Pizzeria and Family Restaurant standing in place of the U.S. Hotel on that Boonsboro corner. At Vesta, you can enjoy a delicious meal and a cozy atmosphere, with very little chance of having your meal interrupted by cavalry.

## EVERY MOUNTAIN TELLS A STORY

Western Maryland is famous for its fantastic state parks and scenic mountain ranges, and even the very names of these mountains emanate with the dramatic stories of some of the earliest and most intrepid Western Marylanders. Some of the mountain names, like Negro Mountain and Polish Mountain, are mired in controversy to this day. I recommend an extracurricular trip to check out those and others, such as Will's Mountain and Dan's Mountain; for today, *Mysteries and Lore of Western Maryland* is going to acquaint you with a few of the most interesting mountain-name tales.

## Evitt's Mountain

Jacob Evart was an Englishman with a broken heart. According to historian Scharf:

*It is asserted that his disgust for civilized life was caused by the frailty, fickleness or falsehood of a woman on whom he had placed his hopes of happiness. When these were wrecked he sought the wilderness.*

We don't know any of the juicy details, but it was bad enough that the well-born Evart left his native land in 1730 and not only headed into the wilds of Western Maryland but also penetrated farther than any other white man had until that point. Evart built himself a lonely cabin there in the hills several miles outside what is now Cumberland. It is said that some years later a man called General McKaig, on hearing the sad tale of "Evart the Englishman," ventured into the mountains and, with efforts associated nowadays with ascending Everest, went in search of the fabled brokenhearted Brit. At the top of the rugged mountain McKaig found signs of Evart's lonely but industrious life: two acres of cultivated land, the remnants of a chimney and some very tasty strawberry plants, which Evart had evidently brought with him from England and which the general is said to have brought down from the mountain and transplanted in Cumberland.

Poor Evart the Englishman's reward for his hermitlike life and disdain for civilization was having a history book comment that he had allowed himself to be "driven from civilization and home and friends [because of a] romantic disappointment which he had permitted to blight his life." And having the mountain where he had wanted to live and die in anonymity named after him—with his name misspelled for that extra kick-a-man-when-he's-down effect.

## Big Savage Mountain

Today, Garrett County's Big Savage Mountain is known for its fantastic hiking. In the 1700s, however, the mountain was the end of the line for white men like Western Maryland's famous "Indian fighter," Colonel Cresap, who would pursue Indians to its perimeter but was too intimidated by the mountain's "impenetrable forest" to go any farther. According to historian Scharf:

This old postcard uses Native American imagery as an evocative depiction of the stories behind the naming of Garrett County's Big Savage Mountain. The caption on the back of the postcard reads, "Hwy. 40 in Western Maryland unfolds many panoramas of breathtaking beauty. This view from Big Savage Mount, is typical. Western Maryland is noted for its Indian legendry." *Author's collection.*

*That mountain was left for years in the undisputed possession of the Indian. The grave of his father was there; it was the ultima thule to which he would retreat.*

*Ultima thule*, by the way, usually means something along the lines of "the farthest reaches of the known world" and is associated with the type of thinking that made ancient mariners believe that if they sailed far enough they'd encounter a bunch of scary monsters and eventually fall off the end of the earth. So it's no wonder the settlers put on the brakes at Big Savage Mountain.

As you have probably already figured out, it was also the settlers who gave the mountain the name "Big Savage," in homage to one of their affectionate little nicknames for the Native Americans. Naming the mountain "Big Savage" also made the white men feel a whole lot better than the more apt "Um, I Think I Hear My Wife Calling Me."

115

## Lover's Leap

The lovers were of the classic star-crossed variety. Her: beautiful, single, Native American, with an overbearing chief for a dad. Him: white, outdoorsman type, young and strapping, raised in the hills of Allegany County. It was love at first gander when the pair met in the lush forests of Will's Mountain. Unfortunately, as you might have guessed, dad the chief objected, but not for the reason you might think. No, it wasn't that the young man was white; it was simply that the boy from the hills was too poor and low class for the daughter of an Indian chief. Dad had great ambitions for his comely daughter and, to the devastation of the young lovers, nixed the affair. In the ensuing argument, the Indian chief was killed. The unhappy couple decided to handle the situation in a sensible manner. They headed straight for the most dangerous cliff on Will's Mountain, clasped hands and leapt off the mountain—straight into the mysteries and lore of Western Maryland.

*Opposite*: The fellow depicted in this vintage postcard of Lover's Leap in Allegany County is having a lot more fun than the star-crossed lovers whose impetuous decision gave the bluff its name. *Author's collection.*

# Bibliography

## Books

Alsop, George. *A Character of the Provence of Maryland*. New York: William Gowens, 1869.

Boyton, Patrick. *Snallygaster: The Lost Legend of Frederick County*. Frederick, MD: Patrick Boyton, 2008.

Browning, Meshach. *Forty-four Years in the Life of a Hunter*. Philadelphia: J.B. Lippincott & Co., 1859.

Cox, William T. *Fearsome Creatures of the Lumberwoods*. Washington, D.C.: Judd & Detweiler, 1910.

Dahlgren, Madeleine Vinton. *South Mountain Magic*. Boston: James R. Osgood and Company, 1882.

Douglas, Henry Kyd. *I Rode with Stonewall*. Chapel Hill: University of North Carolina Press, 1940.

French, Samuel Bassett, and Glenn Oldaker. *Centennial Tale: Memoirs of Colonel "Chester" S. Bassett French*. New York: Carlton Press, 1962.

Harbaugh, T.C. *Middletown Valley in Song and Story*. N.p.: 1910.

Hindes, Ruthanna. *George Alfred Townsend*. Wilmington, DE: Hambleton Printing, 1946

Lowdermilk, Will H. *History of Cumberland, Maryland*. Washington, D.C.: James Anglim, 1878.

Mumma, Wilmer McKendree. *Ghosts of Antietam*. Sharpsburg, MD: Wilmer Mumma, 1997.

Poole, W. Scott. *Monsters in America*. Waco, TX: Baylor University Press, 2011.

Powell, Allan. *Fort Frederick: Potomac Outpost*. Parsons, WV: McClain, 1988.

Rhoderick, George C., Jr. *The Early History of Middletown Maryland*. Middletown, MD: Middletown Valley Historical Society, 1989.

Scharf, J. Thomas. *History of Maryland: From the Earliest Period to the Present Day*. Vol. 1. Baltimore, MD: John B. Piet, 1879.

———. *History of Western Maryland: Being a History of Frederick, Montgomery, Carroll, Washington, Allegany, and Garrett Counties from the Earliest Period to the Present Day; Including Biographical Sketches of Their Representative Men*. Vols. 1–2. Philadelphia, PA: Louis H, Everts, 1882.

Strain, Paula M. *The Blue Hills of Maryland*. Vienna, VA: Potomac Appalachian Trail Club, 1993.

Townsend, George Alfred. *Rustics in Rebellion*. Chapel Hill: University of North Carolina Press, 1950.

Williams, Thomas J.C. *A History of Washington County, Maryland*. N.p.: John M. Runk & L.R. Titsworth, 1906.

## NEWSPAPERS

*Cumberland Evening Times.* "Thirty Years Ago." February 12, 1927.

*Daily News* [Frederick, MD]. "The Jabberwock." April 30, 1887.

———. "Many Local Matters." July 26, 1887.

———. "Many Local Matters." July 19, 1887.

Ellen, Mary. "The Girl About Town." *Daily News* [Frederick, MD], July 27, 1895.

*Frederick Post* [Frederick, MD]. "Heatwave Holds City in Grip as Mercury Mounts." July 22, 1935.

———. "Snallygaster Shot Proves Owl." December 2, 1932.

———. "Snallygaster Story Revived." November 29, 1932

———. "Snallygaster Story Spreads." December 1, 1932.

*Hagerstown Mail.* "The Pate Is Missing." January 5, 1900.

———. "Saw Strange Sight." August 10, 1900.

*Hagerstown Morning Herald.* "Death of Snallygaster Is Reported; Accounts Differ." December 2, 1932.

Harbaugh, Thomas C. "Gapland Castle Crumbling in Ruins." *Frederick Post*, December 1, 1919.

Hunt, J. William. "Across the Desk." *Sunday Times* [Cumberland, MD], December 26, 1965.

May, George. "Dwayyo Could Be a Modern Snallygaster." *News* [Frederick, MD], December 3, 1965.

———. "Dwayyo for Christmas?" *News* [Frederick, MD], December 15, 1965.

————. "Dwayyo Hunt Planned." *News* [Frederick, MD], December 6, 1965.

————. "Dwayyo Monster Is Still Running Loose." *News (Frederick, MD)*, December 1, 1965.

————. "Elusive 'Dwayyo' Still Uncaptured." *News (Frederick, MD)*, December 2, 1965.

————. "Mysterious 'Dwayyo' on Loose in County." *News (Frederick, MD)*, November 29, 1965.

*Middletown Valley Register.* "The Colored People Are in Great Danger." February 12, 1909.

————. "The Great Go-Devil Was Seen in Ohio." February 19, 1909.

————. "Emmitsburg Saw the Great Snallygaster." March 5, 1932.

————. "Hunting the Go Devil Egg." March 5, 1932.

————. "Scene and Incident of Snallygaster's Reign." December 2, 1932.

————. "Strange Monster Mystifies and Alarms Persons Living in South Mountain Section." November 18, 1932.

————. "Two Middletown Men See "Snallygaster" Tuesday Morning." November 25, 1932.

*News* [Frederick, MD]. "Another Old Story." December 1, 1932.

————. "Long-Nose 'Tapir' on the Loose." October 7, 1971.

————. "Runaway Tapir Killed by Truck Near Thurmont." October 19, 1971.

# ONLINE

Cockcroft, Lucy. "Mutant Fish Develops a Taste for Human Flesh in India." *Telegraph*, October 9, 2008. www.telegraph.co.uk/news/worldnews/asia/india/3163501/Mutant-fish-develops-a-taste-for-human-flesh-in-India-html.

Swope Robin. "The Dwayyo, Werewolf of the Northeast." *Examiner.com*, April 3, 2011. www.examiner.com/article/the-dwayyo-werewolf-of-the-northeast.

# INTERVIEWS

Bast, Doug. Interviews with the author, July 2011–April, 2013.

Becker, Paula G. MD. Department of Natural Resources. E-mail message to author, June 3, 2011.

Bender, Mary. E-mail message to the author, March 12, 2013.

Swope, Reverend Robin. E-mail messages to the author, February and March 2013.

Yohn, Jake. E-mail messages to author, February 2013.

# OTHER SOURCES

Brown, W. McCulloh. *Fort Frederick: An Historical Sketch*. N.p.: privately printed, circa 1924.

Cree, Lemoin. *A Brief History of South Mountain House*. Middletown, MD: Mitchell Dodson, 1963.

Dull, David, producer. *Legends*. Cable television series. Hagerstown: Antietam Cable Television, 2002.

Wetzel, George. "The Wizard of South Mountain." Mimeograph. Dundalk, MD, January 1955. Courtesy of Douglas Bast Collection.

# About the Author

Susan Fair lives on the shoulder of South Mountain in Western Maryland. She works for the Carroll County Public Library and the Boonsboro Museum of History. Susan has written numerous articles for a variety of publications, including newspapers, magazines and websites. As a small girl, she used to imagine growing up to drive around and collect strange stories, so in a way, writing *Mysteries and Lore of Western Maryland* has been a dream come true.

CPSIA information can be obtained
at www.ICGtesting.com
Printed in the USA
LVHW010737221220
674782LV00009B/384